ELDERCARE

ELDERCARE

Helping Businesses Support
Employees Who Are Caregivers

SCOT CHEBEN

Eldercare: Helping Businesses Support Employees Who Are Caregivers

© 2025 by Scot Cheben

Library of Congress Control Number: 2025908618
ISBN: 978-1-964686-55-4 (paperback)   978-1-964686-56-1 (ebook)

Although this publication is designed to provide accurate information about the subject matter, the publisher and the author assume no responsibility for any errors, inaccuracies, omissions, or inconsistencies herein. This publication is intended as a resource, however, it is not intended as a replacement for direct and personalized professional services.

Editors: Alexandra Charnin, Jorge David Remy
Cover and Interior Design: Emma Elzinga

Printed in the United States of America

First Edition

3 West Garden Street, Ste. 718
Pensacola, FL 32502
www.indigoriverpublishing.com

Ordering Information:

Quantity sales: Special discounts are available on quantity purchases by corporations, associations, and others. For details, contact the publisher at the address above.

Orders by US trade bookstores and wholesalers: Please contact the publisher at the address above.

With Indigo River Publishing, you can always expect great books, strong voices, and meaningful messages. Most importantly, you'll always find . . . *words worth reading.*

This book is dedicated to Debbie Cheben, a loving wife, mother, and beloved friend.

I miss you every day.

CONTENTS

FOREWORD

When we think about getting our family affairs in order, we often consider childcare and estate planning. But a new role is being thrust upon millions of Americans, one that impacts family affairs and their day-to-day lives: becoming a caregiver for a loved one who is aging or otherwise incapacitated.

Companies have learned how to support their employees when it comes to children, and to some extent, estate planning. But navigating the new challenges presented by an aging population is nascent territory. Being a caregiver impacts your employees' time, mental wellness, and even financial security. Sooner or later, these issues trickle into the workplace, impacting productivity and culture. Worse, the pressure these caregivers experience puts staff retention at risk. Highly skilled, dedicated people, who can't figure out how to balance their new workload and with their employment roles, quit.

Imagine having to jump into a meeting immediately after spending stressful hours bathing and dressing a formerly independent loved one. Imagine juggling your existing workload and other family responsibilities while advocating for a loved one on multiple doctor's visits. Imagine the costs of paying for someone to be present with your elderly parent while you're at work. And then, imagine the paid helper not showing up on the day of your big meeting.

These are just a few of the stressful scenarios that are becoming more frequent as employees cope with aging parents who are losing their independence.

If mental health was a crisis before, expect that crisis to be turbocharged as employees add the responsibility of becoming caregivers to their list—even if that responsibility is limited or on a part-time basis.

That's where you and your company come in.

Helping employees with extended caregiving responsibilities requires understanding what they face from day to day alongside their company role. It means providing them with assistance as part of a broader benefit set.

In *Eldercare: Helping Businesses Support Employees Who Are Caregivers*, Scot Cheben draws from his own broad experience with caregiving, both personal and professional, to help businesses and their employees navigate this new frontier. With clarity about what's at stake, he outlines specific benefits and perks that businesses can offer to ensure employees are well cared for by their employer while they care for their loved ones.

Successful businesses understand the alignment between caring for employees, employee productivity, and overall financial success. Understanding what's at stake and proactively managing the upcoming caregiving explosion is both good business and good sense.

Dive in and start having conversations about caregiving with your employees today. Your employees—and your bottom line—will thank you.

— Carol Roth
"Recovering" investment banker, two-time *New York Times* bestselling author and creator of the Future File legacy and wishes planning system.

ACKNOWLEDGMENTS

If my old schoolteachers knew that I wrote a book, they'd probably say, "What? No way," "Crazy! I don't believe it," or "Really? OMG!"

Writing this debut has been exciting but hard, to say the least. But somewhere between being a kid scraping by in English and publishing this, I found the key to success: maturity and buckling down. Along this path, many people helped me get here, and I'd like to acknowledge them.

To my parents, Karl and Vera: you raised me to care for others and put people first. In today's world, that can be very challenging or even controversial, but as you always said, Mom, "You can be anything you want to be, if you put your mind to it."

This lesson carried me through a lifetime defined by caregiving. I first became a caregiver for my 95-year-old grandfather when I was in high school. We shared a bedroom, and I woke up every night—sometimes twice—to help him to the commode between our beds. Years later and more than 500 miles away, I became the primary caregiver for my 93-year-old father. Those six years set the stage for the hardest chapter in my life. During the last year of my father's life, my wife, Debbie, was diagnosed with stage 4 pancreatic cancer. I cared for them both. Thank the Lord, my Debbie was so strong, or I would have never made it through.

To my amazing wife, Debbie: you supported me through thick and thin. You guided me to the faith we both service today. YOU brought up two amazing kids, Blake and Zachary. You sacrificed so much for our family and never once asked for anything in return (well, maybe a back rub now and then). You taught me the secrets of being frugal while living life to its fullest potential. I can't thank you enough for all that you have done for me and this family.

To my first employers, Richey and Donna: you taught me more about business and real life than any formal education could provide. You have inspired me to work hard, take care of my employees, and appreciate my customers. You were (and are) my second parents.

To Senior Helpers: thank you for educating me on the confusing ins-and-outs of the caregiving field. Owning a business in senior care was very fulfilling, though frustrating at times, and gave me the experience and opportunity to help others.

And finally, a special thanks to the Co-Founders of Senior Providers Network. It all started one afternoon in La Canada where we all met to figure out just how confusing eldercare really is. Admond, my brother from another mother, you and Chris (and Mom) truly showed me what friends are about. I enjoyed all the work we have accomplished, and I appreciate all the knowledge you shared with me over the years.

INTRODUCTION

Life can change on a dime. One minute, you're organizing your wedding registry and, the next, you're juggling work, family, and managing your parent's illness, bills, and well-being from across the country. We'd all like to think we are prepared for surprises like this, the ones that seem to come out of nowhere, but the reality is no one is ever truly prepared. I know my mother wasn't when she was tasked with becoming my grandfather's full-time caregiver, and I certainly wasn't when I became both my father and wife's simultaneous caregiver.

I wrote this book to educate business leaders on how eldercare is currently impacting their organizations, the challenges they and their employees will face in the near future, so they can better understand the risks to their business if they do not proactively integrate eldercare policies and procedures into their organization immediately. Being proactive significantly minimizes the risks aging family members and caregiving have on a business and maximizes the rewards for the business down the road. Not only will eldercare policies and procedures help employees navigate the tricky road of caring for their senior-aged, loved ones, but it will also enable them to return to work faster, under less stress, minimally impacting the business, if at all.

Businesses, in the US alone, are losing billions of dollars annually in lost productivity, absenteeism, and turnover from employees who need to provide care for the elderly. Throughout history, women have provided most of the caregiving. As such, the estimated employment-related costs for mothers providing unpaid care averages $295,000 over a lifetime, based on the 2021 US dollar value, adjusted for inflation.[1] Did you know that businesses pay 8 percent more in healthcare costs due to the added stress and mental health challenges their working caregivers face?[2] About 10,000 people have turned sixty-five every day since 2011.[3] That's almost four million *baby boomers* a year.[4] We are years into this silver tsunami, and we have many more years of growth ahead of us. According to the US Census Bureau, there will be 78 million individuals sixty-five years and older compared to 76.4 million under the age of eighteen."

As such, if your business does not have eldercare policies and procedures in place, it is at risk. Think about it, if your manufacturing worker needs to take a leave of absence for a few months, there are usually other people to step in and fill the gap until they return. But if it's close to the end of your fiscal year, and your Chief Financial Officer has to take a leave of absence for several months to care for their mother, it will cause significant issues for the business. With eldercare policies and procedures in place, you can breathe easy knowing your business is being protected from such issues.

I know it is hard to create change in a business, especially if you have to do it on your own. That's why I wrote this book. Think of it as a guidebook to help protect your business, care for your employees, and continue to grow the corporate culture you've already put in place. Each chapter brings with it a new objective so you and your team can figure out what benefits you currently have in place, which areas need to be shored up, and the best steps to put everything in place.

CHAPTER 1

THE CAREGIVING CONUNDRUM

About 10,000 people have turned sixty-five every day since 2011.[1] That's nearly four million people a year, and we have so many more years of this growth to go. According to the US Census Bureau, "By 2034, there will be 78.0 million people sixty-five years and older compared to 76.5 million under the age of 18."[2]

But many other studies state that companies in the United States are losing roughly more than $30 billion annually in productivity, absenteeism and turnover from employees caring for elderly loved ones. Moreover, caregiving employees are costing your business more than 8 percent – or $13.4 billion – in healthcare costs annually.[3] Yet most businesses have nothing in place to change this. *Why?*

Unfortunately, statistics surrounding senior citizen care needs, solutions, and numbers are consistently outdated. Large corporations such as MetLife, AARP, and Genworth collect and distribute data each year on this exact subject, but few corporations are actually reading it. Without understanding it, businesses cannot make comprehensive adjustments to their eldercare policies, ensuring they continue to lose profits.

From Pyramid to Pillar:
A Century of Change
Population of the United States

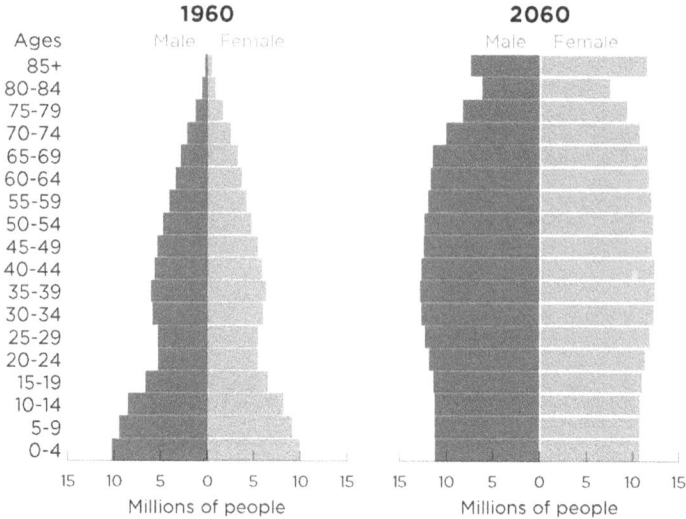

	1960	2060

Source: *United States Census Bureau, National Population Projections, 2017.*

HOW MANY CAREGIVERS ARE THERE?

As of 2024, 73 percent of the United States workforce spends an additional 20 to 30 hours a week caregiving, which drastically increased from 2020.[4]

- In 2023, roughly 11.5 million Americans were caring for loved ones living with Alzheimer's or other forms of dementia. In total, they worked around 18.4 billion unpaid hours in just one year.[5]

- Millennials, born between 1981 and 1996, make up almost 25 percent of the 40 million individuals in the US workforce acting as caregivers.[6]

- The number of unpaid caregivers to aging adults surged from 39.8 million in 2015 to 47.9 million in 2020.

- 82 percent of caregivers care for one adult, while 15 percent care for two adults, and 3 percent care for three adults or more.[7]

WHO IS CARING FOR WHOM?

Despite progressive efforts, there is still a strong disparity between male and female caregivers in the United States. While male caregivers do exist, 75 percent of all caregivers are female.[8] Moreover, female caregivers spend about 50 percent more time providing care than their male counterparts.[9] For instance, according to the National Alliance for Caregiving and AARP, only 24 percent of male caregivers will help a loved one get dressed, and 16 percent will help with bathing. Compare this to the 28 percent of female caregivers who help their loved ones get dressed and 30 percent who will help with bathing, and it's clear to see that female caregivers not only provide the majority of caregiving in this country but are also willing to provide more intimate care than their male counterparts.

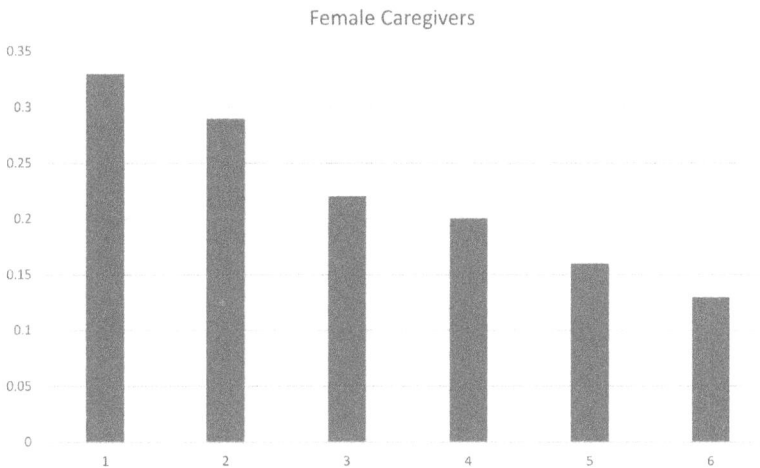

Female Caregivers

Further, many family caregivers find themselves in the *sandwich generation*, a term originally coined by social worker Dorothy Miller in 1981. The *sandwich generation* describes middle-aged employees (between the ages of 30 and 50) who are simultaneously caring for both their children and elderly parents.[10] For instance, among employees in their 40s, 65 percent have a child under 18 and a parent aged 65 or older that they are helping financially. Of those in their 40s with children over 18, nearly 21 percent have provided financially for both their children and their parents.[11] As such, caregiving employees, especially those in the *sandwich generation*, can have long-lasting and far-reaching impacts on the businesses they work for.

Adults in their 40s are the most likely to be in the 'sandwich generation'

% who have a parent 65+ and have a child younger than 18 or have provided financial support to an adult child in the year prior to the survey

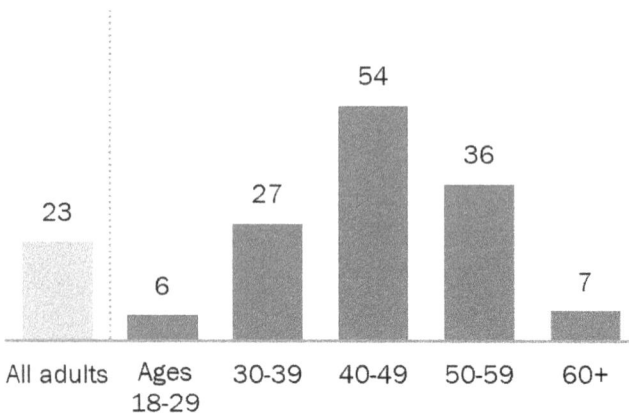

Source: Survey of U.S. adults conducted Oct. 18-24, 2021.

PEW RESEARCH CENTER

THE DEFINITION OF CAREGIVER

care·giv·er / ˈkerˌɡivər/

1. A family member or paid helper who regularly looks after a child or a sick, elderly, or disabled person.

A caregiver assists with a loved one's activities of daily living (ADLs) during a chronic (ongoing) or acute (sudden onset) illness or disease. They can be a friend, family member, associate, or a trained professional, paid (formal) or unpaid (informal).

Conditions Requiring Care	
Acute	*Chronic*
• Develops suddenly and last a short period, a few days or weeks. Cure is common. • Example: Influenza • Acute conditions in most cases are caused by a virus or an infection. It can be brought on by an injury resulting from a fall or accident.	• Develop slowly and may worsen over time —months or years. Cure is rare. • Example: Alzheimer/Dementia • Chronic conditions are often caused by poor nutrition, lack of physical activity, alcohol abuse, etc. Genetics can also play a role as we age. People are more likely to develop one or more chronic conditions like

BECOMING A FAMILY CAREGIVER

If you have an elderly or ill relative that requires special home care, you may have to step into the role of caregiver if there is no one else available to provide such care. While learning how to become a family caregiver can require a great deal of time and patience, there are a few family caregiver resources mentioned throughout this book that you can draw from to make your transition less stressful and more productive.

Responsibilities of the Family Caregiver

Unfortunately, very few individuals have a plan for what they will do as their parents age. When something happens to your senior loved ones, it can feel like you have just a few minutes to figure out what to do. However, the family caregiver is akin to being the CEO of a company. They must make decisions on behalf of their loved one, ensuring to act in the same manner, or at least as close as possible, as their loved one would if they had the capacity to do so. This job is stressful, overwhelming, and thankless, yet it is also one of the most rewarding and comforting roles a person can have.

In fact, between 2021 and 2022, the average caregiver spent roughly 28 percent of their day providing eldercare.[12] On average, they spend around 3.6 hours a day caregiving and performing such duties as:

- Medication management: Ensuring their loved one takes their medications correctly, on time, and in the correct dosage.

- Food preparation: Making sure food is ready to cook or making it easier for their loved ones to cook independently if they want.

- Personal hygiene assistance: Helping them with bathing and other personal hygiene tasks to ensure they are able to maintain their dignity and ease the burden on other family members.

- Emotional and social support: Providing their elderly loved one with support so they can maintain their independence and dignity and improve their quality of life.

- Transportation: Helping their loved one move safely and comfortably within their home and community, especially if they have a disability.

- Financial accountability: Performing support tasks like paying bills or preparing taxes on behalf of their loved one.

- Household chores: Handling day-to-day tasks like cleaning, laundry, shopping, and childcare.[13]

Other responsibilities can include:

- Providing nutritional support.
- Monitoring the individual's health.
- Managing home safety.
- Communicating with healthcare professionals on the individual's behalf.
- Planning activities for the individual.
- Providing pet care.
- Managing medical appointments.
- Offering respite for family members.
- Advocating for the individual's needs.

Benefits of Becoming a "Primary" Family Caregiver

The "Official Primary Family Caregiver" is an unofficial title that applies to the person in charge of caring for a senior loved one on a daily basis. As the point person, you will have the legal authority to get up-to-date information about the condition of your family member's health. You will also have the responsibility to advocate on their behalf and make the necessary decisions that are in his or her best interest.

What Are the First Steps to Becoming a Family Caregiver?

The first step to becoming the official family caregiver is learning everything you can about your family member's condition. You may also want to recruit other family members into the caregiving role to share the responsibility with you.

Once you know everything you can about your family member's condition, the next step is to find out exactly what your relative's medical insurance will cover, and, consequently, what it will not cover. The more information you have concerning their coverage, the better. Additionally, you will need to contact each of their physicians to inform them of your caregiving role.

Gathering Legal Documents for Your New Position

After you have officially established yourself as the caregiver, you will need to make your title or status legal. If your relative is able to, they must sign an Advance Directive and Health Care Proxy form. These documents will give you the legal status you need to make official decisions on your relative's behalf without the interference.

In addition to the Advance Directive and Health Care Proxy forms, you will also need to have Power of Attorney. The Power of Attorney (POA) is a legally binding agreement that gives you the authority to act for another person in legal or financial matters. However, an adult child cannot create a POA for their parent and name themselves the agent without their parent's permission. The parent must be mentally capable to sign the document. Once the parent creates the POA, they will choose a particular person to act in their best interest.

The POA document can be made ahead of time because it will state the exact date it is meant to go into effect. Moreover, there can be different styles of POA documents. Some may appoint one person to manage the individual's medical needs, with another person to manage their financial. POAs are incredibly important to have in place prior to your loved one needing one, ensuring a seamless transfer of authority.

Draw on All of the Available Resources

There are several state and federal resources you can draw upon while transitioning into your new position as official caregiver that will make the journey much smoother. For instance, the Family Caregiver Alliance and the National Family Caregiver Support Program are excellent state programs that will help you navigate the challenges that will surely crop up.

Other resources you can lean on include:

- Adult day care centers
- Respite care
- Meals on Wheels
- Financial assistance

However, even with all of the legal legwork sorted out, it is important to recognize that you may still have a great deal of trouble adjusting to your role as an official family caregiver.

THE ELDERCARING EMPLOYEE

Typically, when an employer asks an employee if they are caring for a loved one, the answer they are most likely to hear is, "No." Most employee caregivers do not want their employers to find out about their caregiving responsibilities for fear of repercussions.

This may seem ludicrous to the non-caregiving employer, but most caregivers are notoriously terrible at self-reporting. Even when asked point-blank, employee caregivers will want to hide their new role outside of work to ensure their employers do not think they are being distracted.

Unfortunately, keeping this from your employer only adds fuel to the fire. Just look at what almost happened to Sharon:

Sharon was well-known at her company for her ability to stay on top of her workload. No matter what her supervisor threw her way, she was able to turn it in well before the deadline. Then, she started coming into the office late a few mornings a week. Then, she began leaving work early or missing a day here and there. Given her reputation, her employer and coworkers saw a pattern emerging, and noticed a decline in her work accomplishments and physical appearance. One day, she was even seen sleeping at her desk beyond the scheduled lunch break. It didn't take long before rumors were circling around the office about Sharon's possible drug use.

Sharon's supervisor, Casey, requested that she come to his office to discuss his concerns. Casey asked all the right questions but wasn't able to figure out why the office's top performer was slacking off. All Sharon offered Casey was an apology, assuring him that things would change.

A month went by and nothing changed. It wasn't until right before Sharon was going to be fired that she finally confessed that she was caring for her ailing mother. Her mother's Parkinson's diagnosis prevented her from getting out of bed in the morning. She had also begun to need help moving around the home and feeding herself as the tremors progressed. The late nights and early mornings had left Sharon sleep-deprived and unable to maintain her usual workload and performance at the office. While many of her peers believed Sharon had a substance abuse issue, she was simply exhausted and overwhelmed by taking care of her mother and continuing to be a full-time employee.

Family Caregivers Think They Can Do It All.

The demands on caregivers can be overwhelming, especially when trying to do it all without the support of others. Oftentimes, the support just isn't there, and rarely is a break or multi-day respite an option.

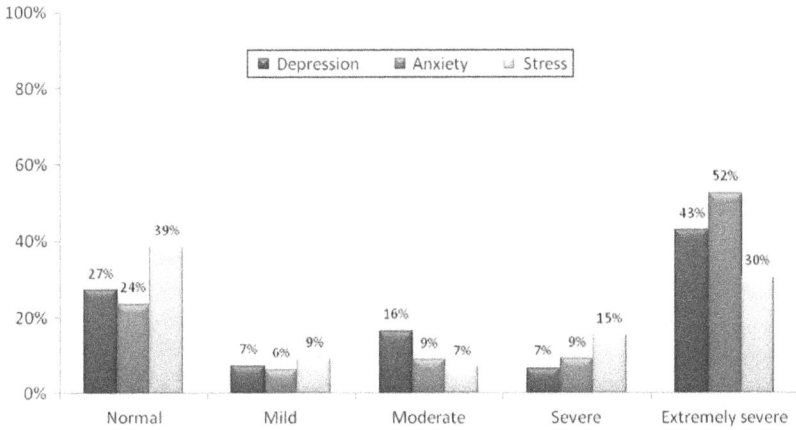

However, when the caregiver gets sick, they are no good to anyone.

The mental and psychological health of a caregiver is greatly affected by the burden or responsibility that they take on. Caregivers have higher levels of stress, anxiety, and depression, which greatly impacts their own health, as well as that of family members who are sharing the responsibilities.[14] Studies have shown that between 40-70 percent of caregivers show significant signs of depression.[15] Many of these caregivers meet the criteria for major depression, and the impact of caregiving only increases when the individual is responsible for a person with dementia, whether they are in a managed care facility or residing at home. In fact, according to a 2022 report, more than 50 percent of dementia caregivers experience major depressive symptoms.[16] However, most caregivers look after their ailing loved ones in their own homes because of the exorbitant costs of alternative housing. Thus, restorative and enjoyable "me time" is infrequent, leading to overwhelming and potentially chronic diseases, substance abuse disorders, and even suicide.

Furthermore, caregivers often feel frustrated and worried when the health of their elderly loved one begins to decline. This transition can lead to a loss of self-identity, diminishing self-esteem, and heightened sleep issues. Moreover, employee caregivers can feel less effective in both their personal and professional lives, and less in control of both. A report by the National Library of Medicine (NIH) has shown that there is a direct relationship between chronic stress and cognitive decline in caregivers, which directly affects their health and well-being.[17] It's no wonder most caregivers report that their own health is compromised due to the daily stress caregiving places on them.

It is crucial for businesses to realize that caregiving duties not only affect the employee, but they directly affect the business, their clients, and the other employees. Business leaders don't often comprehend the significance of this until someone in a senior management role becomes a caregiver themselves. For instance, it was only when the head of human resources for a major corporation became her aging mother's caregiver that she realized the plight that was befalling other employees. While for many people taking care of their parents or elderly loved ones is a privilege, there is still a tremendous amount of stress even in the best situations. Thus, it is imperative that employers and businesses take part in alleviating additional stress when they can.

US citizens born between years 1946 and 1964 are the largest generation of people alive in the US, and they have reached, or are about to reach, retirement age. Providing care to this *baby boomer* community has become a full-time job for many American families, especially when many baby boomers are caregivers to elderly loved ones themselves.

As mentioned above, it is estimated that 48 million Americans provide unpaid caregiving assistance to their elderly family members annually. In 2021, the cost of this unpaid caregiving was estimated to be around $600 billion. This number is more than what is spent on nursing home and traveling home health care combined.[18]

There are several common stressors that arise in caregiving:

- Changes in relationship dynamics
- Being on-call 24/7
- Disagreements
- Cognitive impairments like dementia or Alzheimer's

THE IMPACTS OF EMPLOYEE ABSENTEEISM

Caregiving, in general, substantially affects businesses. Employee absenteeism hurts every business, and trying to replace employees who have to quit their positions to provide full-time caregiving can have serious financial consequences for any business. For instance, the costs to replace employees who resign because of their caregiving responsibilities have been estimated at over $3 billion annually.[19] Moreover, full or partial-day absenteeism and workday interruptions cost businesses around $5,600 annually *per caregiver*.[20] This number is much higher among caregivers of elderly adults with significant care needs.

Getting employees back to work quickly without stress should be paramount for businesses. The world of eldercare is fragmented and confusing for most caregivers. There is never enough guidance to go around. At the beginning of their caregiving role, life can feel suddenly disorienting and overwhelming. Providing employees with the right resources will help ensure that this transition goes smoothly and that they can get back to working proficiently, saving the business money in the long run.

WHAT IS THE SANDWICH GENERATION?

As discussed in the prior chapter, the term "sandwich generation" refers to individuals who support both their children and their parents. These groups differ wildly in the kinds of support they need, adding additional strain to their caregivers. While both men and women are equally as likely to become part of the sandwich generation, the caregiving roles for sandwich generation employees tend to be split nearly sixty-forty, with most female employees taking the lead.[21]

Not long ago, parents supported their children until they gradu-
ated from college or found gainful employment. They weren't tasked
with providing support for their own parents until much later in life—
typically after the older parents had the adequate resources to support
themselves, even if that meant being moved to an assisted-living center
or nursing home.

Today, however, the burden on the sandwich generation has grown
considerably. Not only are couples having children later in life, but parents may not have saved enough for retirement or had their savings
depleted through things like medical treatments or bad investments.
According to a 2021 study by the Pew Research Center, the sandwich
generation is made up of around 23 percent of US adults. Additionally,
54 percent of this age group has both a parent sixty-five years of age or
older and is either raising a child under 18 years of age or has an adult
child they are helping financially. These numbers are much higher than
other age ranges. For instance, only 7 percent of individuals over the
age of 60, 36 percent of individuals in their 50s, 27 percent of those in
their 30s, and 6 percent of people under 30 are in a similar situation.[22]

SANDWICH GENERATION AND THE EFFECTS OF EMPLOYEE ABSENTEEISM

As more of the sandwich generation cares for their families and juggles
the responsibility of supporting both their children and their elderly loved ones, the more their work may get interrupted. When more
of this employee's work time is interrupted, the harder it will be for
them to complete their projects, stay on track, and try to improve the
business. Furthermore, an employee who is struggling to juggle their
responsibilities is more likely to suffer from their own health issues. All
of these consequences can be disastrous for your business.

Effects on the Business and Their Employees

While all employees miss work occasionally, the number of planned and unplanned absences grows considerably when individuals must provide financial support to their immediate families and their elderly loved ones. When employees miss work or have difficulty concentrating on their work tasks, they can worry about their position in the company, leading to further stress and feeling overwhelmed. For instance, with the high cost of living in the United States, more and more families live in multigenerational households, and now grandchildren are sharing the responsibility of caring for their grandparents with their parents.

Are Millennial Caregivers Becoming the New Sandwich Generation?

In 2017, I attended a three-day human resources conference where I spoke to two human resources directors about their eldercare needs. After I was done chatting with one of the directors at a midsize company, I turned to her colleague to find out if she had any eldercare questions for me. The colleague told me that the staff at her company was primarily made up of millennials and didn't need any eldercare support. I smiled, having heard this same story a number of times before, and went on to explain that the highest divorce rate in the United States occurred between 1979 and 1981, with 5.3 divorces per 1000 marriages.[23] In 2000, the divorce rate was down to four divorces per 1000 marriages. Most children born in these eras came from split homes and with grandparents who were significantly involved in their upbringing. As such, these grandchildren would likely feel obligated to care for them now.

The woman nodded at my explanation and then smiled. Before turning to leave, she told me she would contact me when she thought her company needed help. But the next morning, this same woman came running up to me, obviously upset. In her hand was a resignation from a millennial employee who had just informed her she needed to resign to take care of her aging grandmother.

While the media has promoted the idea that millennials are self-involved, the truth is that they may actually be the generation that needs to care for both their aging parents and grandparents and, in some cases, their young children as well. Today, there are roughly ten million millennials who are care companions or who provide some type of substantial support for their elderly parents, grandparents, or relatives.[24] In fact, these ten million adults represent nearly 25 percent of their entire generation, and this number is expected to rise.

Millennials are now the largest generation, outnumbering baby boomers near or into their retirement years, and, because of their size, this generation will arguably be the one sandwiched between two other generations that may not have to carry so heavy a burden.

Are You Prepared?

- More and more individuals are tasked with caring for ailing and aging family members.

- The additional stress that caregiving places on a person can cause them to begin performing poorly in their work.

- The "sandwich generation" is responsible for supporting both their children and elderly loved ones, putting a tremendous amount of strain and stress on their personal and professional lives.

- Creating eldercare policies and procedures to protect and support your employees is the best way to enable your employees to get back to work, improve their performance, and protect your business from being negatively impacted by their absenteeism.

CHAPTER 2

FINANCIAL BURDENS FOR ELDER CAREGIVERS

Social Security is a federal insurance program that provides benefits to retired people and those who are unemployed or disabled. However, when a person is not working, they and their employer are not contributing to Social Security. Thus, the cost of caring for our elders not only affects the family caregiver in terms of lost wages but can also affect the entirety of the American economy. In fact, the total income, Social Security contribution, and private pension losses that occur because of caregiving could range from $283,716 for men to $324,044 for women over a lifetime.[1]

To try and offset these personal and national economic burdens, a caregiver might try getting paid for their work, which would allow them and their employer to pay into Social Security. For instance, aging parents can create a personal care agreement between you and them if they have the means to pay you directly from their savings or some other asset. Additionally, if you are caring for a parent who is eligible for Medicaid benefits, you may be able to get payment for the care you provide under a federal Cash and Counseling Program" and similar state programs that are offered under different names.[2] Family Caregivers can also be paid directly out of insurance benefits such as long-term care insurance and Veteran's Administration (VA) benefits.

Interestingly, 14.3 million Americans are caring for veterans or current members of the military.[3] Considering that many veterans suffer from illnesses and conditions unlike their civilian counterparts, this places an even greater strain on caregivers, especially if they are required to become caregivers earlier and earlier in life.

Recent studies by groups like the AARP (formerly known as the American Association of Retired Persons) have discovered that caregivers may spend upward of 26 percent of their income to take care of their elderly loved ones, with some caregivers spending even more.[4] For example, minority groups like Hispanics and Latinos actually spend about 44 percent of their income taking care of their seniors.[5] Moreover, most family caregivers are women, though the number of men assuming the role is growing, which places additional burdens on these individuals for taking on non-traditional roles. This type of mental labor can compound a caregiver's depression symptoms. In fact, one study found that upward of 70 percent of caregivers may be suffering from depression. However, men are much less likely to seek treatment.[6]

Additionally, as the only generation that may be forced to take care of their parents, grandparents, and children at the same time, the pressure is on for millennials to succeed in their careers and life. When this pressure and stress is added to the burden of being a caregiver, millennials are likely to experience increased financial strain and depression that can be hard to overcome.

Whether millennials are truly the next sandwich generation doesn't really matter. It is clear they've become the primary care companion force in the United States. This means that despite earning less than their parents and experiencing an incredibly high cost of living, millennials shoulder far greater financial burdens because they must raise their own children while also taking care of their parents and grandparents.

In total, it is costing these sandwich generations nearly $10,000 and 1,350 hours a year to care for their parents and children.[7] While children tend to be more costly, the sandwich generations spend more of their time with the aging and time is money, causing a significant financial burden on the caregivers and their family.

According to a study on female caregivers in the US:

- 33 percent of working women had to decrease the number of hours they could work.
- 29 percent passed up taking a new assignment, training, or job promotion assignment because of their caregiver role.
- 22 percent took a leave of absence to provide care.
- 20 percent moved from full-time positions to part-time employment.
- 16 percent of female caregivers quit their jobs to provide their caregiving services.
- 13 percent of these women retired early to meet the expectations of caregiving.[8]

In terms of financial support, 68 percent of family caregivers support their elderly loved ones, which comes from their own employment income.[9] This is about $190 billion in out-of-pocket expenses every year.[10] Not only is this excessive, but it also impacts how families pay for their own expenses or whether they are able to help other family members in need of financial assistance. For instance, many family caregivers are forced to reduce their working hours or change their schedules to ensure they can assist their loved ones. Others may even have to switch jobs or quit work altogether.

Given this potentially tremendous financial toll, it is important for them to find every resource for financial assistance. While this might sound like an overwhelming task, there is plenty of support available throughout this book.

SAVING FOR RETIREMENT

Far too many people in America are not prepared for retirement. Baby boomers and seniors have reported that their biggest financial challenge was planning for retirement. Younger millennials seem less concerned about retirement than their older counterparts despite having higher debts and fewer assets. As such, millennials are less likely to have a retirement account, be able to purchase their own home, and choose to acquire stocks than people their age were just a few decades ago.[11]

If you were to think of retirement as a stool, personal savings, Social Security benefits, and pensions make up the three legs beneath the base. Each one is important, yet many people rely on just their Social Security benefits or just their pensions to prepare for retirement. However, Social Security retirement benefits are only intended to supply 40 percent of a person's salary.[12] Additionally, it is important to realize that if an employee takes longer than a month to settle their caregiving responsibilities, it can affect their retirement savings because neither the employee, nor their employer, are paying into the benefit for that period.

If Americans would like to continue living their current lifestyle while working, they will need additional cash in the bank. Yet, 57 percent of Americans have less than $1,000 in their savings.[13] According to the Economic Policy Institute (EPI), "Nearly half of families have no retirement account savings at all."[14] In fact, the median value of a 401(k) account for someone sixty-five and older is about $89,000.[15] That's not much to live on when spread out over twenty years. Moreover, Social Security benefits and pension benefits are constantly coming under pressure and cannot be relied upon as this country continues to age.

According to the Social Security Administration, as of August 2024, the average retiree receives just $1,783.55 monthly from Social Security.[16] That's a little over $21,000 a year. And the median private pension was only $11,040 per year, according to the Pension Rights Center (state, local, and federal pensions were higher).[17] Furthermore, only a few people can collect both social security benefits and private pensions, which won't really move the needle for them. They will need at least ten times that amount in savings to make a significant impact on their retirement.[18]

WHY AREN'T PEOPLE SAVING FOR RETIREMENT?

Americans list a number of reasons why saving for retirement is difficult, including debts, low wages, and college tuition. Although these things can stretch our budgets, they don't make it unreasonable to still save for retirement.[19] Insufficient planning, retail marketing, and personality weaknesses can also contribute.

Good Jobs with Good Benefits Encourage Retirement Savings

Having a good job that offers a workplace retirement plan, such as a 401(k) or 403(b), can significantly aid your retirement savings efforts. These plans allow you to contribute a percentage of your salary (up to annual contribution limits) toward your retirement, making it easier to budget for your future. Typically, these contributions are made with pre-tax dollars, which offers two key benefits:

1. It reduces your taxable income.
2. It allows your retirement savings to grow tax-deferred.

This means you won't pay taxes on contributions or their growth until you withdraw the funds in retirement. However, it is important to note that when you do take distributions from these tax-deferred retirement plans, they will be taxed as ordinary income. Additionally, if you withdraw funds before the age of 59.5, you may be subject to a 10 percent federal income tax penalty, with some exceptions.

By taking advantage of these workplace retirement plans, you can more effectively save for your future while potentially lowering your current tax burden.

THE COST OF SENIOR CARE

Are you among the many members of the never-aging baby boomer generation or the sandwich generation caring for elderly parents who don't live nearby? Or perhaps they are close, but work keeps you too busy to get over to check on them daily? Do you think that having an aging parent live with you in your home might be much cheaper than moving Mom or Dad into an independent or assisted-living facility?

Whatever plan you choose, you must be prepared for miscellaneous expenses, especially if your loved one doesn't have a pension or personal savings and will depend on you for support. Even if your family member moves into your home full-time, that will still cost *something*.

The cost of senior care will vary dramatically depending on where you live. To combat the confusion around these costs, the Genworth Cost of Care Survey details the national average cost of senior care in every category. It lists the states with the least and most expensive options to help family members find a place to meet their—and their aging relatives'—healthcare needs at an affordable price.

Given the varying costs, many individuals may purchase long-term care (LTC) insurance, which is designed to help pay for long-term care costs not covered by health insurance, Medicare, or Medicaid.

Home Care

Home care includes homemaker and home health aide services that are either done at home or in an assisted-living facility. In 2023, the national median monthly cost of homemaker services was $5,720, while the average cost of home health aide services was $6,292.[20] Home care services that are covered by LTC insurance usually include home-making, companionship, meal preparation, and medication remind-ers. They also will typically include personal care services such as bath-ing, dressing, and grooming.

Adult Day Care

Adult day care centers provide elderly individuals with daytime su-pervision and social activities in a structured setting. Some adult day care centers will also offer more intensive health and therapeutic ser-vices for their patients. The national median cost of adult day care was $2,058 monthly, which is more than half the price of the monthly av-erage for assisted living, and a third of the monthly average for home care, with Alaska, North Dakota, Vermont, Maine, Idaho, Montana, and New Mexico ranking as the most expensive on the list.[21]

Assisted Living

Assisted-living facilities offer residents the opportunity to live in an apartment-style unit, with personal care and individualized services like meal delivery, when necessary. These facilities offer daily struc-tured activities and care like social and recreational activities and basic health services. The cost of assisted-living facilities depends on the level of attention the resident requires and the state in which it is located. In 2023, the national average spent on assisted living was $5,350 monthly. However, the averages differed significantly from state to state, with the minimum being around $3,800 a month and the maximum around nearly $8,700 monthly.[22]

Nursing Home Facilities

Nursing homes are generally for people who may need a higher level of supervision and care than an assisted-living facility can provide. Nursing homes offer residents personal care, room and board, observation, medication, therapies and rehabilitation, and skilled nursing care twenty-four hours a day. As of 2023, the national average for a semi-private room was $8,669 monthly, and over $9,700 monthly for a private room.[23]

Are You Prepared?

- Planning for retirement takes more than just saving money. The retirement stool is made up three legs: Social Security benefits, pensions, and personal savings. As the cost of living increases, so does the demand on US citizens to have enough to retire on.

- If your elderly loved one is eligible for Medicaid benefits, you may be able to get paid to take care of them through a federal Cash and Counseling Program." You can also get paid directly out of their long-term care insurance or VA benefits, if they have them.

- Taking care of your loved one, whether you have them move in with you, hire home care assistance, or place them into adult day care, assisted living, or a nursing home, you need all the financial support you can find.

CHAPTER 3

HOW CAN BUSINESSES HELP CAREGIVERS?

The best way to help your employees is to be proactive. Give your business, its practices and policies, a once over every so often to ensure they are meeting employee needs. If you don't know what your employees need, try surveying them. It can be as simple as asking, "By a show of hands, how many of you are caring for, have cared for, or know someone who cared for an aging loved one?" during a company meeting or Christmas party. If you see a lot of hands in the air and know you don't have the strongest—or any – eldercare policies, you'll know there's a potential problem brewing. You might have a problem on hand or will soon, which you will have to figure out.

Another approach would be to ask your HR department to pull a few items from the employee database and add them to a spreadsheet:

- Total number of company employees
- Employee genders
- Their hourly pay or salary amount

Gathering your employees' gender will tell you what kind of exposure you might experience if your employees start taking on eldercare roles. As we know from previous chapters, it is much more likely that a female employee will leave work to care for a loved one than a male employee. So, if you have more females than males on your team, you may lose more team members due to eldercare responsibilities than a team that was made up of more males.

In addition to these items, you will also want to know the average hourly rate of your company. If you don't have that number, use the national average wage, which is $35.46 an hour in America.[1] Then, you take the average number of hours per year that employees spend away from work. It's reported that 15 percent of the workforce is caring for a loved one.[2]

Once you know this information, there is a simple calculation to figure out how much your business could potentially lose in productive wages—which we know exposes the bottom line for any business. First, take the average number of hours per year that employees spend away from work, which is usually around one work week (or forty hours), and multiply it by the total amount of the workforce that is caring for a loved one (15 percent).

Example: A company has 560 employees and 15 percent are caring for a loved one. So, your calculation will look like this:

560 employees x 0.15 = 84

84 employees x 40 hours a week = 3,360 hours of lost productivity

3,360 hours x $35.46 (the average hourly rate in the US) = $119,145.60 in lost productivity wages!

Losing this much money from your bottom line can greatly impact your business. Even if you think that you'll never lose the entire 15 percent of employees at once, it can still negatively affect your profit margins. For example, if you lost just 8 percent of your employees and their productivity because they had to take care of a loved one and had the same 560-person business, that's almost $64,000 in lost productivity wages.

PROVIDING EMPLOYEES WITH THE RESOURCES AND TIPS THEY NEED

Employee benefits programs that include eldercare services are usually not as robust as the demand employees have for them. Recently, companies have begun allowing employees to donate some of their paid time off (PTO) to coworkers who have family emergencies. A PTO donation or leave sharing is a step in the right direction for companies as these policies tend to be a lifesaver for some employees.

Is this enough? Ask your employees what *they* think.

I can guarantee you, it's not. As baby boomers age out of employment and millennials and Gen Z begin to take their place, eldercare policies need to take the forefront of any business planning. As explained in Chapter 1, millennials are the children of the generation with the highest divorce rates in America. Many of those children were raised by their retired grandparents and are now leaving the workforce to take care of those loved ones. Moreover, they may also have dependent children to look after and financially support, making employee caregiving policies necessary.

When employees are facing a difficult eldercare situation, they're in a state of crisis. They're focused on getting their loved one the care they need and trying to problem solve in a situation they don't have a solution for, creating an immediate panic. Because of this, they are not necessarily focusing on making the best decisions, whether at home or at work. Offering your employees senior care assistance can help alleviate these stressful situations, decrease distractions, and improve their work-life balance.

Integrating senior care resources into your employee benefits program is a surefire way to improve business functions. Understanding the statistics behind why an eldercare Employee Assistance Program (EAP) is necessary helps provide for effective HR decisions:

- 53 million Americans informally care for an elderly loved one.

- Over 38 million of these individuals continue to work while caregiving.

- 53 percent of caregivers are either late to work, leave early, or have to take time off to caregive.

- 15 percent are forced to reduce their hours.

- 14 percent have to take a leave of absence.

- 7 percent are unable to take promotions when offered.

- 4 percent lose their job benefits entirely.[3]

Beyond caring for elderly parents, the aging workforce also cares for their brothers, sisters, and spouses. In truth, these individuals are staying in the workforce longer to make up for the losses to their retirement because of their caregiving responsibilities. In 2022, there were 58 million individuals aged 65 and older.[4] This number is expected to rise dramatically to 82 million by 2050.[5] Eldercare is thus an unavoidable issue that must be addressed in a business's policies and procedures to alleviate stress for the owner, CEO, and employee. One way to help reduce your employees' stress, decrease absenteeism, improve their happiness, and help them maintain a healthy work-life balance is to choose an eldercare EAP program.

NATIONAL FAMILY CAREGIVER SUPPORT PROGRAM

Another significant resource that your team can tap into is the National Family Caregiver Support Program (NFCSP). Founded in 2000, the NFCSP offers grants to states and territories based on their share of the population over the age of 70.[6] This program helps employees provide the best possible home care to sick or elderly relatives who need their help. By utilizing the NFCSP, you are giving your employees the assistance they need to not only provide their family members with excellent care but also get them back to work full-time without losing any money for the business.

The NFCSP offers a wide range of special services to caregivers and those they care for. The program provides your employees with full access to these services and the information they need to access and make use of the services. The more information you have about these incredibly important services, the easier it is to make sure your loved ones are as comfortable as possible.

Who Is Eligible for NFCSP?

Under the 2016 Reauthorization of the Older Americans Act, caregivers who qualify for NFCSP services include:

- Informal caregivers aged 18 years old or older, or other adult family members, who are

caring for individuals aged 60 years old or older

- Individuals of any age who have Alzheimer's disease and similar conditions
- Relatives, not parents, aged 55 years or older who are caring for children under the age of 18
- Relatives, including parents, aged 55 and older who are caring for adults with disabilities between 18 and 59[7]

Once you apply, the NFCSP will notify you of the services you qualify for under your company's particular program. As such, it is important to notify the NFCSP immediately if your organization's needs change so they can ensure your employees are getting all the benefits available to them.

Individual Counseling, Support Groups, and Training

Giving part-time or full-time care to an aged or ill family member is a serious task. The NFCSP is authorized to provide a range of special counseling and training services, both on an individual and group basis. This will help you become a more attentive and effective caregiver to the one you care for. These services are also designed to help you deal with the strain of being the primary or sole caregiver to an aged or ill relative who can no longer look after themselves.

Top Quality Respite Care

Few people can care for an elderly or sick relative all by themselves. Sometimes, taking a break to regroup is necessary. Without eldercare benefits, many employees cannot take this kind of time away from their loved ones. As such, having respite caregivers to turn to is more than necessary. NFCSP can help direct you or your employees to high-quality respite care services.

Access to a Wide Variety of Supplemental Services

The NFCSP can also provide you with a wide variety of special supplemental services designed to give you the extra support you require. These supplemental services are provided on a limited basis to complement the care your loved ones already receive. Contacting your local organization is the best way to learn what services the NFCSP can offer your specific company and employees.

OTHER ORGANIZATIONS THAT CAN HELP

While the NFCSP is a specialized program designed to aid caregivers who are also employees, there are other organizations that can help employees manage their caregiving role. However, these benefits come from outside of the business organization. For instance, Meals on Wheels can provide fresh meals to individuals and families in need. Local churches may also offer Durable Medical Equipment (DME) loaner services. If your loved one needs a shower stool, walker, or wheelchair and their insurance won't cover these expenses, one of these organizations may be able to loan you one.

IT'S TIME TO BE PROACTIVE

In addition to providing your employees with eldercare benefits, you might also think of offering them a planning tool like Future File (FutureFile.com). Future File is a comprehensive system that helps individuals and their loved ones discuss their end-of-life requests and organize important information, policies, and documents to assist with medical and other emergencies, aging issues, and even their passing. By having this system available to employees, there will be fewer disruptions to your employees' personal and professional lives and, thus, your business. Future File is a cost-effective benefit that shows your employees you care about the issues affecting their families, easing their stress and improving their productivity.

HOW OTHER COUNTRIES ARE CARING FOR THEIR ELDERLY

By 2050, the amount of elderly that will require care will dramatically increase to four times the current amount.[8] Furthermore, about half of these individuals will need some form of dementia care, which astronomically increases the burden on family caregivers. While many focus countries lack proper elderly in-home care, along with proper facilities to address this growing number, like the United States, they have begun prioritizing problem-solving such issues.

- Japan: As of 2024, Japan had the highest percentage of people over the age of 65.[9] To help these individuals and their caregivers, Japan has several programs and policies, such as:

- Long-term care insurance system

- "Better Life Better Place" for the elderly and children program[10]

- Home and community-based care

- Employment opportunities and the extension of the retirement age

- Japan's Post "Watchover Service"

- Prevention programs that focus on health promotion and disease prevention for the elderly

- Incorporating age-friendly features in housing and urban design

- Playing crucial roles in enabling active aging and community-based engagement[11]

- Italy: Coming in second after Japan, Italy's population over the age of sixty-five comprises about 22.8 percent of the entire population. As such, a lot of government spending is geared toward providing assistance to these individuals, including service vouchers, daytime centers, and qualified assistance for home care.[12]

- Netherlands: The Netherlands has created an entire village called "Hogeway." Half the population of Hogeway suffers from dementia-related issues and are assisted by the other half of residents who have been trained as caregivers. This experimental program gives those suffering from dementia the feeling of living a regular life amid shops, cafés, and other stores that make up the village.[13]

- United Kingdom: Roughly six million people in the UK assist relatives, friends, and neighbors who need support. Called "carers," these individuals often have full or part-time jobs to support themselves while helping to take care of others.[14]

However, some countries are still struggling with how to care for their elderly population. For instance, China has a significant need for eldercare assistance but is struggling to find resources.[15] They do not have an organized association of caregivers, so, for the most part, family caregivers are the ones shouldering the burden of taking care of their elderly relatives.

Caring for Loved Ones with Dementia

When it comes to caring for family members with dementia or dementia-related diseases, some countries have managed to tackle these difficult issues while maintaining dignity and love.

- India: The Alzheimer's and Related Disorders Society of India (ARDSI) visits the homes of low-income seniors who suffer from dementia and related conditions to provide proper treatments, as well as to the elderly individual's family.[16]
- France: In France, individuals who suffer from dementia can visit a "Snoezelen room," which is meant to calm them during violent or angry outbursts. The Snoezelen room offers them a peaceful, soothing atmosphere to relax in, complete with a waterbed, soft lighting, and even bubbles from water tubes.[17]

SHOULD WE RELY ON THE GOVERNMENT?

Unfortunately, most politicians look at the world in a certain way and rarely agree on anything. We are a reactive society governed by a reactive government. In other words, we don't create policies or regulations until something happens. We are constantly trying to quickly fix issues rather than thinking ahead and stopping them before they have a chance to impact us. For example, consider 9/11: We knew our country's airport security was not evolving at the same rate as the evil in the world. Instead of creating more robust policies and updating our technology, it took a significant destructive event to do something about it. The same can be said for the way Brady's Law impacted how firearms are sold, or how Megan's Law was introduced to help parents identify sex offenders living in their neighborhood. A horrible act had to happen for these laws to come into legislation.

Are You Prepared?

- 15 percent of employees will have to provide eldercare support to their aging relatives. If your business is mostly made up of female employees, this percentage can increase dramatically.

- Losing this many people from your company for even just one week out of the year can lower your company's productivity significantly, severely decreasing your business's bottom line.

- Employers need to create eldercare benefits for their employees to help alleviate their employee's stress, support their caregiving, and get them back to work quickly.

- There are a number of caregiver benefits to offer employees, but the most robust is the National Family Caregiver Support Program (NFCSP). Contact your local office to learn how they can help your organization.

CHAPTER 4

BENEFITS AND BROKERS

For many millions of people, caring for elderly relatives is a full-time job on top of the full-time job they already hold. Imagine your employee moonlighting as a live-in nurse for an unspecified number of hours while trying to maintain optimum performance on their job. The fatigue that inevitably sets in will affect the quality of their job performance.

Even though many people in such a position remain dedicated and hardworking employees, their absences and caregiving responsibilities will prevent them from functioning at a high level, costing their companies millions of dollars per year. Providing eldercare services and resources to your employees is an investment that enables your company to continue achieving its productivity and profitability goals.

Becoming a caregiver is a hardship for your employees that will only continue to increase over time. Our population is aging and the pressure on your employees will take an enormous toll physically, emotionally, and financially. If you do not currently offer your employees eldercare benefits, or your benefits are not comprehensive, now is the time to make those changes. Eldercare services and resources should be included in your standard employee benefits package.

When my father had a stroke, I had just one day to prepare before I was thrust into the life of a caregiver. I had to figure things out for myself, relying on Google as most people do, since my company had no resources. Unfortunately, Google confused me even further because I wasn't asking it the right questions—I didn't know what the right questions were to ask. Even today, given all that I know, and how Google and AI have evolved, the answers to my questions are still vague and ambiguous.

For instance, I recently told AI, "I need help caring for my elderly father." The response it gave me was, "If you need help caring for your elderly father, consider assessing his needs first, then exploring options like in-home care services, adult day programs, respite care, or even assisted-living facilities depending on his level of care required; communicate openly with your father about his needs, and reach out to local aging agencies or support groups for guidance and potential financial assistance programs."

Clearly, this response is not detailed enough, especially for someone just getting into caregiving and with no prior experience. Yes, you should explore options like in-home care services, but there are different types of in-home care companies, and not all of them are created equally. As for seeking out local aging agencies or support groups, these are usually just temporary fixes, and you may even need to qualify before you know if you are eligible for them.

Utilizing Google and AI isn't necessarily a bad thing, but if you don't know what you are looking for, how will you know which advice is sound and which should be avoided? By providing employees with eldercare benefits and resources, companies can alleviate this frustrating experience and enable their employees to get back to work faster after taking on their caregiving role.

HOW EMPLOYEE BENEFITS AFFECT TOTAL COMPENSATION

As more companies offer unique employee benefits packages to try and attract top-tier talent, the cost of these benefits has plateaued around 30 percent. Benefits aimed at boosting workplace productivity and attracting the best employees comprise a significant percentage of a worker's total compensation at different positions throughout different industries.

DETERMINING THE VALUE OF AN EMPLOYEE BENEFITS PACKAGE

A typical employee benefits package will make up about 30 percent of an employee's total compensation.[1] For example, an employee who earns $65,000 a year will typically also have benefits amounting to about $20,000 annually. These benefits will include health coverage plans (about $3000 for singles and $6000 for families), life insurance policies, short- and long-term disability, and retirement plans.

Newer packages also include dental plans, student loan reimbursement, and assistance with eldercare. Each benefit adds to the cost of the total compensation package. Here, an employee receiving $65,000 in base salary will in reality cost the company about $85,000.

MANAGING THE COST OF EMPLOYEE BENEFITS

While benefits packages continue to represent a significant portion of an employee's total compensation, it is important for businesses to manage the overall cost of employee benefits. The challenge is to provide competitive benefits packages to continue to recruit top-tier talent, but at a reduced cost to the company.

Control Healthcare Costs

Healthcare costs are perhaps the largest driving force of the cost behind employee benefits. Providing competitive healthcare plans to workers means offering plans that cover prescription medication, in- or outpatient treatment, and other types of care. To manage the cost of these benefits, employers need to look for the specific packages that your employees need. Consider the population breakdown of your workforce—is there a good mix of millennials and those from Generation X? Or are they mostly middle-aged? Knowing the demographics of your workforce can help you spend wisely on healthcare benefits.

Solicit Employee Feedback

It's difficult to know what benefits your employees need unless you ask them. You can request feedback in anonymous surveys, in-person interviews, or any other method you find most productive. This will help you get rid of benefits programs that employees aren't fond of and employ the ones they do.

Implementing High Return on Investment Benefits.

Not every employee perk has to be expensive. Some of the most valuable benefits packages are relatively inexpensive to set up. The key here is to go beyond the upfront cost of benefits and consider the return on investment (ROI). For example, did you know that for every $1 that goes into implementing an EAP, allows the business to enjoy $3 return on average?

MOST POPULAR EMPLOYEE BENEFITS TODAY

Sixty percent of job seekers today will focus on the employee benefits packages offered before accepting a job.[2] In fact, four out of five workers would prefer to get a new benefits package over a pay raise.[3] As more job seekers place emphasis on comprehensive benefits, businesses must adapt their current offerings to accommodate those needs.

Your business will find it challenging to attract top talent if you aren't providing popular benefits packages that most job seekers are looking for. Listed below are some of the core components an employee benefits package should include, which will resonate among the current workforce and attract and retain top talent.

COMPREHENSIVE HEALTH INSURANCE

Due to the high volatility that surrounds healthcare in the United States, more workers are seeking stable and comprehensive health insurance packages from their employers that offer quality care for themselves and their families. Moreover, workers are also expecting their health insurance package to cover dental expenses, some cosmetic procedures, and long-term care.

FLEXIBLE VACATION AND TIME OFF

Providing employees with time off is one of the best ways to keep a workforce productive. Many workers are looking for a company that places employee well-being over the bottom line and encourages employees to avoid burnout.

Vacation time is a popular and essential employee benefit to provide to employees. Most businesses offer 15-20 days of paid vacation

time per year. However, some businesses have implemented more lu-
crative vacation packages, while others also provide up to a week of
paid volunteer time to encourage employees to engage in charitable
activities.

PARENTAL LEAVE

As businesses recruit a younger workforce, they are bound to experience new parents among their employees. An important benefit for
employees to provide is an inclusive parental leave package that allows
workers, both male and female, to take time off to care for their newborn child. In fact, Netflix offers a full year of paid parental leave to
their employees,[4] while Spotify offers six months of paid leave with a
flexible return period.[5]

PERFORMANCE BASED BONUSES

Many workers desire recognition for the outstanding work they do
for their employer. Performance bonuses don't just come in money or
gifts. Opportunities for personal development have become popular
components of an employee package. For example, Asana provides ex-
ecutive and life coaching services to their employees outside of work
time.[6]

CHOOSING THE RIGHT EAP PROVIDER

Choosing the right EAP provider to support your employees is a critical decision. If you invest in an EAP program that's well under budget
yet doesn't meet employee demands, then the investment isn't worth it.
You could find a spectacular EAP program with high-quality solutions

that fit perfectly in budget, but only if you conduct the research necessary to find the right provider for your company. There are many factors to consider for choosing the right EAP provider. The right plan will help your business to avoid costly mistakes and improve employee well-being, productivity, and increase your company's potential ROI.

EVALUATE YOUR COMPANY

It's helpful to compile all the data you can find on both your company and employees before you try to determine which benefits are a better fit for your company. Send out polls and surveys to employees to dive deep into where their true needs and shortcomings lie. Ask questions like: "What are your most pressing needs for support? How often are you away from the office and why? Are there any benefits we fail to offer that you need? If so, what are they?"

If you currently offer workplace benefits, analyze the utilization rates and data for those to determine whether they are necessary, or if they can be replaced with something more applicable to the particular team you have and the business you run. Once you've gathered all necessary data, you can make more effective, data-driven decisions.

DETERMINE YOUR NEEDS

The range of employee benefits are quite wide, but once you've analyzed your data, you then can determine what your most pressing employee needs are. For instance, do your employees need an eldercare EAP program to help them with caring for their aging loved ones? Are they in need of more paid leave because they are burned out and exhausted? Did you see an influx of requests from employees searching for mental health services or counseling?

If you discover that a great deal of your employees attribute their absenteeism to caring for their elderly parents, you'll know your next step is to find a high-quality, user-friendly eldercare EAP program. Making this connection and doing something about it will help directly solve your employees' biggest pain point and improve their workplace performance.

RESEARCH AVAILABLE EAP PROGRAMS

Another way to figure out which EAP is best for your company is to speak to the companies you've partnered with or other companies you're familiar with in your industry to determine which EAP program is best for your company. You can even look into the providers they use for their employees benefits and ask for their reviews.

Asking Google and using the resources in your area are also great ways to find available EAP programs for your company. If you decide you need help finding the right EAP program, you can hire an employee benefits broker. These brokers are often educated on legislative changes happening in health care, industry standards, and the top EAP providers to choose from.

Now that you know exactly what your company and employees need, and you have a list of EAP providers you're interested in, it's time to do a deep dive on each potential vendor. Make sure to research things like:

- How long have they been in business?
- What kind of medical professionals do they use?
- How highly rated are they in their reviews and customer testimonials?

It's important to partner with an EAP provider who offers the solution you need and is an expert in their field. While you're doing a deep dive on each potential vendor, you'll also want to look into the vendor's background, the business owners, and their mission. Only after doing this kind of deep research can you be sure you have found the perfect EAP provider for your employee benefits.

WHY ELDERCARE SERVICES ARE NECESSARY EMPLOYEE BENEFITS

Employees juggling an elderly loved one's physical and emotional well-being, medical needs, and finances on top of their job obligations are understandably overwhelmed. Unfortunately, EAP programs that include eldercare benefits are usually not as robust as the employee demand is for them. For example, did you know that:

- 5 million Americans informally care for elderly loved ones.
- The average lost income for an informal caregiver is $303,880.
- 57 percent of informal caregivers report they have no choice but to perform clinical tasks.
- 40 percent of them are in high-burden situations (21+ hours per week caregiving).
- 1 in 4 caregivers spend 41+ hours per week caregiving.
- Live-in caregivers spend 40.5 hours per week caregiving.[7]

The point of offering employee benefits is for them to be utilized so that companies can keep their employees productive. Yet the least sought-after benefit employers are looking into today is eldercare employee benefits. With the staggering statistics above, one has to wonder why this is the case? Well, for one, healthcare costs are skyrocketing, so the cost of medical insurance is climbing. Clearly, it's the most expensive benefit that businesses pay for. Traditionally, it's been medical, dental, vision and 401(k)s, but brokers today are being creative and offering things like tuition reimbursement, wellness programs (including financial), prepaid legal, identity theft and pet insurance. In fact, the number of larger employers offering identity theft protection rose 56 percent and pet insurance is up 80 percent.[8]

WHY ELDERCARE BENEFITS SHOULD BE MORE PREVALENT

When the Family Medical Leave Act (FMLA) was originally introduced, the decision-makers creating benefits packages were much more focused on meeting the needs of parents. So, maternity leave and child care resources were more necessary at the time. Now, however, today's organizational leaderships are getting older and aging managers are likely facing their own eldercare issues. Moreover, these employers can see that the younger generations are caring for an older family member, like a parent or grandparent. As such, they are beginning to increase their focus on eldercare benefits.

According to the National Study of Employers, larger organizations are far more likely to offer eldercare resources, like Dependent Care Assistance plans, and referrals than smaller ones.[9] In fact, 64 percent of employers with 1,000 or more employees offer eldercare resources, versus the 37 percent of employers with just 50 to 99 employees who do.[10]

Caregiving for the aging can be both challenging and rewarding, but make no mistake, it is one of the most thankless professions in America. Businesses and leaders need to be more proactive about the needs of caregivers to ensure they have the support necessary to continue to care for an aging society without damaging their employer's bottom line.

CHOOSING THE RIGHT ELDERCARE BENEFITS

Eldercare benefits should give your employee access to resources and professionals in every industry to ensure that their loved ones are being taken care of. When employees have this kind of peace of mind, they are able to continue working and improving their productivity. Yet, as mentioned above, pet insurance is offered more frequently than eldercare benefits and is one of the fastest-growing voluntary employee benefits.[11]

The average annual cost of pet insurance in 2023 was about $676 per year for dogs and $383 per year for cats.[12] Companies like Amazon, Athenahealth, and Ben & Jerry's all offer their employees some form of pet insurance.[13] Some companies are even subsidizing a percentage of their employee's costs, and several are actually paying as much as 100 percent of their employees' pet insurance premiums.

While over 68 percent of US households own a pet, there are 40.4 million unpaid caregivers supporting adults ages 65 and older. On average, family caregivers are spending $7,000 in caregiving-related out-of-pocket expenses every year. The annual cost of owning a dog is $1,750 and the annual cost of owning a cat is $1,350. Which number should your business want to reduce more?

If you only offer your employees family health insurance, maybe some kind of vision and dental, and pet insurance, what are they supposed to do when their parent falls and breaks a hip? How can you help those employees? More than likely, these employees will need to take time off work to caregive. They will feel much more supported in doing so if they know their organization is behind them.

Are You Prepared?

- Find the right EAP provider by learning exactly what the people currently working for you need out of their benefits package.

- Make your employees feel seen and heard by personally inquiring into their needs.

- Pet insurance is great and all, but eldercare benefits are more important for your employees and your business's ability to remain productive as more and more employees take time to care for their aging loved ones.

CHAPTER 5

HOW TO GET THE MOST OUT OF YOUR BENEFITS BROKER

Benefits brokers, sometimes called advisers or consultants, can be valuable resources which save your organization a lot of time and energy when choosing benefits packages for your employees. But to ensure you have a positive experience with your benefits broker, you should approach the relationship in a professional, transparent manner that places your goals at the forefront.

CHOOSING THE RIGHT BROKER

If you don't select a broker or firm that aligns with your company's needs, it will be very difficult to maximize the return on investment (ROI). It is important to research various brokers and brokerage firms to ensure their expertise and knowledge align with your needs. For example, it is a good idea to see if the benefits brokerage has created benefits packages for companies with employee populations that are similar to yours. If they haven't, then they might not know what your organization needs and thus wouldn't be a good fit to work with.

When hiring a benefits broker or firm, it is important to consider your company's size, the specific benefits your team requires, any legal or compliance standards that must apply to your business benefits, and all other concerns that will affect the employee packages you can offer. Picking the right benefits package is arguably the most important step in having a successful relationship with your benefits broker, so be sure not to rush through the selection process.

COMMUNICATE FREQUENTLY

Open communication is the foundation for any good relationship, including the one you have with your employee benefits adviser. While you probably won't need to speak to them every day or even every week, it doesn't hurt to keep a running tally of questions that you can periodically send to them.

Remember to observe how responsive your broker is and whether they can provide prompt, effective solutions for the challenges you present to them. Good communication is a sign that your broker is engaged and invested in their relationship with you. It can be a good idea to schedule a regular check-in call with your broker—perhaps once a quarter—so they can talk to you about changes to your policies or new benefits options.

ASK YOUR EMPLOYEES FOR SUPPORT

While mired in the data, numbers, and policy decisions, it's easy to forget that employee benefits packages are made for people. It doesn't matter how cost-effective your benefits package is from a business perspective: If it is not providing the advice and assistance your team members need, it won't be an effective policy.

Additionally, it's important to request as much help as possible from your benefits broker to ensure that your employees understand the benefits the broker is offering. From training modules and showcases to technical support, your broker (or their organization) should have professional resources available to assist your employees directly.

HR PROFESSIONALS: HOW TO GET THE MOST FROM YOUR EAP PROVIDER

You already know the importance of EAP providers for making sure your team members are healthy, happy, and engaged at work. But if you are wondering how successful your EAP program is and whether you are getting your money's worth, it's a good idea to review the EAP program. If you don't keep an eye on it, it may become a seldom-used resource that isn't actually helping your employees as it should.

Here are four ways to ensure your EAP resources are fully taken advantage of by your employees:

1. Track and Analyze the Data

Most EAP providers will provide you with information about your company's use of their resources. While privacy regulations prevent them from providing specific information, they can track general trends about how your employees are using the EAP resources in different areas, like substance abuse, family concerns, and financial management. If you see that employees are heavily utilizing a particular area, you can speak to your EAP provider about increasing the resource available in that area. You can also look into decreasing resources in an area that isn't being utilized.

2. Talk to Your Team

While data and reporting can provide a good general overview of what's happening with your EAP program, nothing is better than actually conversing with your employees to see what they think about it. It is important to make sure your company culture is seen as a safe space to speak freely. If it isn't, your employees might not feel able to speak honestly. However, when they do, you can glean valuable insights on what is and isn't working with your EAP program.

Don't forget to log these conversations so you can refer to them later for future planning sessions and ensure that you are making decisions that align with the requirements of your employees. If scheduling in-person meetings with each employee isn't feasible, you might consider sending out company surveys as an alternative to ensure that you can continue to put your employees' needs at the forefront of your EAP offerings.

3. Schedule Periodic Updates and Reviews

Just because you've obtained and implemented an EAP program doesn't mean your work is done—an EAP is not a "set it and forget it" type of resource. Schedule regular meetings with representatives across all divisions and levels of your company so that everyone is on the same page and can provide their own feedback on the organization's EAP program. Based on these check-in meetings, you can create new goals and milestones to help make your EAP even more effective.

4. Encourage Employee Community

An EAP program is extremely valuable to help employees deal with personal, medical, and family issues, but sometimes the best way to assist employees is by facilitating support from their peers. If you know that several employees are dealing with similar challenges—such as taking care of elderly parents—you might build a group or community within your organization that can exchange information and experiences, as well as resources with one another. In addition, you can also incorporate these types of resources into company correspondence, such as a quarterly newsletter to ensure anyone who needs the information is able to get it. The goal is to create communities that do not infringe on any one employee's privacy. So, remember to make these communities completely voluntary.

FOUR SIGNS YOU MIGHT NEED TO CHANGE YOUR EMPLOYEE BENEFITS PACKAGE

Is your company getting a healthy ROI from employee benefits? Do you have low utilization rates, or are your employees unhappy with the resources offered? As explained above, when it comes to employee benefits, the solutions offered must be tailored to employee needs and then evaluated periodically.

As employee needs change over time, so will your benefits packages. It is crucial to your company's productivity and company culture that the employee benefits package is continuing to produce an ROI for your company overall. Below are four signs it might be time to change up your employee benefits package and how you can tailor your benefits package to fit employee needs, and thus increase ROI.

1. Utilization Rates are Low

While it may seem like a given that employee benefits are there to help employees, many companies forget to analyze the usage rates to see how much employees actually utilize their resources. The first thing to do, then, is review and analyze your employees' utilization rates. What percentage of people are using employee benefits? What specifically are they accessing? Who in the company is accessing it?

Just like with EAP programs, if you discover you've invested into benefits that have a low utilization rate when compared to your employee count or the other benefits you offer, it may be time to switch things up. Working with EAP providers who assist in the reviewing process also helps.

2. ROI Isn't High Enough

If your company invests a lot of time, resources, and money into employee benefits that are only being used by a small percentage of employees, it might be time to reconsider your benefits package. Something to factor in while assessing ROI is that typical employee benefit utilization is in the single digits, somewhere between 3-6 percent, but well-designed and effectively communicated programs can achieve higher rates, potentially reaching the teens or just below 20 percent. However, if your company's utilization rates are anything under 10 percent, your company likely doesn't have good ROI. If your utilization rates and ROI are low, it's time to change your employee benefits package to fit your employee's needs better, increase your ROI, and improve company productivity.

3. Employees Aren't Satisfied with Current Benefits

One of the best ways to understand employees' needs is to listen to them and ask what they need directly. What benefits do they love? Are there any benefits they need to have that you're not offering? Do they have any complaints about the ones currently available?

If their needs aren't being met by your current benefits, it's time to change them. Create and distribute surveys to your employees and figure out where their pain points lie, what's decreasing their productivity levels, and what benefits they'd like to see. Then, you then can create an effective employee benefits package to fit employee needs.

4. Excessive Employee Use of Leave/PTO

It may be time to change your employee benefits package if you've noticed increased use of leave or PTO. If many employees are taking time off for the same reasons (and you offer no benefit to support them in that problem), implementing a new EAP program that caters to their needs is a surefire way to decrease employee absenteeism and increase your company's ROI.

Many of the difficulties employees face aren't unique. It's common to see much of employee absenteeism stem from similar large problems, such as eldercare. For instance, 37.1 million Americans cared for an elderly loved one between 2021 and 2022 alone.[1]

As you can see, partnering with an experienced employee benefits broker and actively engaging with employees can significantly enhance your ability to select the most appropriate benefits package. Brokers bring valuable expertise in navigating the complex benefits landscape, offering insights into market trends, and negotiating favorable terms with insurance providers. Meanwhile, direct communication with employees provides crucial feedback on their needs and preferences. This two-pronged approach allows you to design a benefits package that not only aligns with your company's budget and goals but also addresses the diverse needs of the workforce.

Remember, a good employee benefits package is one that is relevant to the employee's needs, provides financial security or well-being support, is accessible, and can positively impact their work-life balance. Having a comprehensive health insurance, retirement savings plans, paid time off (PTO), flexible work arrangements, and opportunities for professional development are great places to start. But providing eldercare benefits to your employees will ensure they feel supported in their new role as a caregiver, have the time they need to learn how to juggle this new role, and provide them with a work-life balance that avoids burnout, which leads to more productivity and an increased bottom line for your company.

Are You Prepared?

- Choose a benefits broker or firm that aligns with your company's needs to maximize your ROI.

- Ask your employees what benefits they actually need and which ones you currently offer that they don't utilize.

- If your company utilization rate of employee benefits is lower than 10 percent, you need to change the benefits package to better fit their needs.

CHAPTER 6

RESOURCES AND TIPS FOR FINANCIALLY BURDENED CAREGIVERS

Taking care of your aging loved ones is not for the faint of heart. It is a big responsibility and can become a huge undertaking if you are unprepared. Add to this any kind of financial instability, and caregiving becomes even more cumbersome. Unfortunately, I understand this additional stress and fear all too well. My father had Champagne taste on a beer budget, which only added to my stress caring for him. He has more expenses than income, and it was just a matter of time before he ran out of money. When your aging father is craving $27 per pound of special cheeses, it's hard to deny it. I was lucky enough to be able to help without having to ask for money, but not everyone is and companies need to understand that.

TAKING CARE OF AGING LOVED ONES WHILE CONTINUING TO WORK

One of the most difficult decisions for family caregivers of elderly parents is how to take care of them when they have a job. The idea of putting your loved ones in senior care centers has considerable drawbacks, but the idea of giving up your career is not a pleasant thought either, especially if you have other individuals and children to support. To figure out your options, you need to consider two things:

- Ability: Can I help my parent around the house with their physical and mental needs?

- Affordability: Can I or my parents afford appropriate care while I'm at work? If I quit, will I need to get paid for being a family caregiver?

After answering both questions, you need to determine what it is your elderly loved one actually needs. Consider the following factors:

- What is the state of their mental and physical health?

- What is their current physician's prognosis?

- Ask yourself what, if anything, is lacking in their current situation?

- Is it viable for your loved one to continue living at home?

- Do they want to live with other seniors in an assisted living or nursing home facility? Or some other kind of community that can provide a residence and the care they need?

The truth is, it is going to come down to what your parents need and what they want. Your role is going to be assessing what their situation is today so that you can address what they need tomorrow. However, because caregiving lives on a spectrum, even if your parents are on one end or the other, you will still need to take care of the things in between.

My father, for example, asked me not to put him in an assisted-living facility. While I did my best to keep him home and hired a caregiver to come by a few days a week to help, this situation required my father to take care of himself as best he could when he was alone. It was a tenuous situation, made even more so because I didn't live close by and there are only so many times you can ask a neighbor to check in before you start to feel like a burden.

MINIMAL ASSISTED CARE

If your parents need some help around the house during the day with things like cleaning, laundry, dinner, in-home services can address those needs. Other options for minimal assisted care include adult daycares, where your parents can engage in social activities and meal time before going back to their residence for the night.

Moving In

Whether you move into their home, or they move into yours, living together is an option when more help is needed than an in-home services provider can offer. When you are home from work, you will take over the caregiving role. This option requires considerable changes to your life but allows you to continue working.

If this is something you are considering, make sure to check with Medicare or Medicaid to see if your loved one qualifies for additional assistance services. You can also look into their pension or retirement benefits to see if either include any elderly assistance.

Moreover, many elderly individuals value social interactions quite highly, especially with people their own age. Having them visit senior centers or moving into a care facility may be the best answer. In any event, there are ways you can care for your parents while keeping your job. It will take considerable adjustment but there is plenty of senior home care assistance out there if you just look.

WHY YOU SHOULD BECOME A PAID CAREGIVER

If you are one of the millions of Americans attempting to hold a full-time job while also being a family caregiver to your aging loved ones, you can be compensated for your time. By becoming a paid caregiver, you can get both the income and assistance you need to make sure you are able to take care of your financial responsibilities and that your parents get the care they need.

EXTERNAL AGENCIES CAN BE UNRELIABLE

Another benefit of becoming your family's paid caregiver is that you can't always rely on, or afford, an outside senior home care agency to give your loved ones the care they require. The resources at external senior home care agencies are often stretched thin, or their costs have increased. Either way, once it is impossible for them to care for your loved one, you must figure out how you can take over that primary caregiving role.

INCREASED INCOME

Many individuals become paid caregivers simply because they cannot afford another option. Yet becoming a paid caregiver can actually improve the situations of both you and your aging loved one. For instance, in the case of an emergency, paid caregiving allows you to have your own money to purchase medication, food, safety equipment, and other necessities. It also affords you the opportunity to have more money to spare for your personal expenses.

PERSONAL CARE AGREEMENTS AND DIRECT PAY

Whether you want to become a paid caregiver or not, having a personal care agreement or caregiver contract between you and your loved one is important. As explained in an earlier chapter, having a personal care agreement in place is especially useful if you will be getting paid directly from your loved one's savings or some other asset. In addition, having your particular arrangement in writing will help you, your loved ones, and any other third parties understand what is expected and what their responsibilities will be when the contract goes into effect. To learn more about personal care agreements and caregiver contracts, you will need to consult an attorney who specializes in them. Your attorney will review the contract and ensure meets all the necessary conditions for your situation and location.

MEDICAID CASH AND COUNSELING PROGRAM

Many elderly individuals are eligible for Medicaid. If so, you may be able to get paid as their caregiver under the Cash and Counseling Program. This special program provides payments to the primary family caregiver so that you can meet all of the expenses that come from the care you are providing. Also, even if the loved one you are caring for doesn't qualify for Medicaid, it is important to check if there are other programs in your state that offer something similar.

INSURANCE OR OTHER BENEFITS PAYOUTS

Another way you can receive income as a caregiver is to see if you can be paid directly out of your loved one's insurance benefits. For instance, if they qualify for monthly in-home care benefits, the benefit will pay the provider directly. As such, if you are the one providing these services, you may be able to have their insurance pay you directly instead. Other benefits that offer some financial assistance for eldercare include:

- Long-term care insurance
- Life insurance
- VA benefits

Again, having a personal care agreement in place will ensure that nothing gets in the way of your loved one's care. The first place to start is with professional assistance if you can afford it. Many families opt to hire an attorney who specializes in eldercare law, but a less-expensive option may be a geriatric care manager, assuming you do not need legal help as well. Geriatric case managers can still be costly, but they are a great solution for seniors who do not have special needs. Moreover, depending on the insurance your loved one has, the cost of a geriatric case manager could be partially covered.

Thrift Stores: For equipment that your insurance company doesn't cover, check out local thrift stores, particularly those run by churches or religious organizations. You will find that thrift stores can provide equipment and items for several different needs at a considerable discount, which will enable you to maintain your budget.

Utility Company: Many people are unaware of this, but the special equipment you need to effectively caregive can increase your electric bill. As such, your utility company will likely have special programs and discounts that can help offset these additional energy costs. Plus, if you live in an area prone to natural disasters like hurricanes, tornadoes, and earthquakes, or that has power outages often, notifying your utility company of your caregiving status will encourage them to place you at the top of the power restoration priority list.

For family caregivers, finding every economic advantage is crucial when taking care of loved ones in the home. By following some of the tips below, you can save a considerable amount for the day-to-day needs of your loved one.

LIFE INSURANCE CAN HELP YOUR LOVED ONE LIVE INDEPENDENTLY

Many people decide they don't want their life insurance policy anymore and choose to sell it. The law permits the policy owner to sell their life insurance through a broker to a third party. However, while the seller will get more for the policy than the cash surrender value the insurance company offers, it will be much less than what the policy's beneficiary would have gotten upon their death. The amount that the life insurance policy is sold at to the third party is known as a life settlement. Moreover, the policyholder must be 65 years of age or older to be eligible to sell their policy this way.

When you begin planning for your future, taking out a life insurance policy makes a lot of sense. You are focused on protecting the people you love if something should happen to you. But what happens when people are not around anymore? In such a case, you might not see the sense in continuing to pay the premium and decide that a life settlement is the best alternative.

In other instances, an elderly loved one may not see the benefit of having life insurance, especially after they have retired and are starting to live off their retirement income. If after all that careful planning, they realize their retirement income is not enough to provide for the lifestyle they have become accustomed to or had in mind, they can sell it. This may help instead of suffering through retirement. This money can be used to subsidize their retirement income.

In life settlement transactions, the life insurance policy holder gets a cash payment and ownership of the policy, as well as its premium costs are transferred to the buyer. Then, when the insured individual dies, the third-party buyer receives the death benefits. What's more, if you are worried about a single individual receiving your death benefits, you can also enter into a life settlement with a life settlement provider. With licensed life settlement providers, though, there is a question of privacy; as such, working with a proficient settlement broker is key.

Even though the life settlement actually benefits the third-party buyer more than the insured individual, if you need additional capital, this is a viable way to secure it. Moreover, this is an option for individuals who need money now to be able to pay for a caregiver.

HOME EQUITY CONVERSION MORTGAGES (HECM) AND REVERSE MORTGAGES

If you own a home, you know that your home equity is the most important asset you can have, and it is the only part of the property you truly own. Thus, if you need more income to support your retirement, you can trade or sell your home equity for cash. Additionally, reverse mortgages don't require the loan to be repaid instantly, monthly or even in installments. Instead, the loan only needs to be paid back fully when you exit the house. This allows you to build your equity back up over time and continue to pass the home over to your heir.

HOW DOES A REVERSE MORTGAGE AFFECT SOCIAL SECURITY?

Many people refuse to pursue a reverse mortgage because they fear for their social security. But a reverse mortgage does not have any effect on your social security. Your social security is based on the amount of money you have acquired in your time working. So, you can still qualify for a reverse mortgage in your retirement and continue to collect the social security amount you earned while working.

REQUIREMENTS FOR A REVERSE MORTGAGE APPLICATION?

Before a lender will let you apply for a reverse mortgage, you must:

- Show you are at least sixty-two years old.
- Prove that you have enough equity to clear your debt.
- Have occupied the residence for at least six months or more.
- Show proof from the government that you have never been in public debt before.
- Prove you are financially equipped to maintain and care for the property.

Remember, changes are constantly being made on how to apply for a reverse mortgage. Before beginning the application process, make sure you speak to a qualified attorney or bank representative for up-to-date instructions.

VETERAN AFFAIRS AID AND ATTENDANCE AND HOUSEBOUND BENEFITS

Government websites are notoriously difficult to navigate. If you aren't sure of what you are looking for exactly, you will most likely have a hard time finding it, and trying to call the government for answers is even harder.

According to the VA government website, veterans or survivors who qualify for a VA pension and require another person's help and presence, or are housebound, may be eligible to receive these additional monetary benefits. The Aid and Attendance and Housebound benefits are an additional payment and cannot be paid out unless the individual is eligible for a VA pension. Moreover, because the Aid and Attendance and Housebound benefits will increase the veteran or survivors pension amount, individuals who are not eligible for the basic VA pension because their income does not qualify might be eligible for a pension at these higher rates. However, a Veteran or surviving spouse cannot receive both of these benefits at the same time. It's one or the other.[1]

My recommendation to family caregivers is to familiarize yourself with the VA website and collect the following documents before contacting your local VA regional office.

1. Discharge/Separation Papers (DD-214). If you don't have a copy of these documents, you can either fill out an SF 180 or, you can visit http://www.archives.gov/veterans/military-service-records and follow the instructions on the website. Keep in mind that requesting a DD-214 takes approximately two weeks, and, if you also check the "medical records" box, it could take even longer to locate because they will not send you anything until they have everything organized. However, you do not need medical records to apply for these benefits, just a copy of your military records (DD-214).

2. A copy of Marriage Certificate and all marital information.

3. A copy of the Death Certificate (if you are the surviving spouse of an eligible veteran).

4. A copy of current Social Security benefit award letter. If you do not have one in your possession, you can request it from a local office or online).

5. The applicant's net worth including bank accounts, CDs, Trusts, Stocks, Bonds, Annuities, etc.

6. Any insurance premiums, medications, medical bills or other non-reimbursable medical expenses.

7. Physician orders that include sufficient detail to determine whether there is disease or injury producing physical or mental impairment, loss of coordination, or conditions affecting the ability to dress and undress, to feed oneself, to attend to sanitary needs, and to keep oneself ordinarily clean and presentable. This report should also indicate how well the applicant gets around, where they go, and what he or she can do during a typical day. In addition, it is necessary to determine whether the claimant is confined to the home or its immediate premises.

8. Banking information on a voided check for Direct Deposit of Aid and Attendance monthly payments.

Once you've collected all necessary documents, you must complete either the

- VA Form 21-526: If you currently have a disability that results from an injury, disease, or an event that occurred in military service, and/or

- VA Form 21-534: If you're applying for VA benefits as a surviving spouse or child of a deceased veteran.

When filling out the forms, always verify that the mailing address is correct, because any mistakes could delay benefits. In addition, make sure you mail your applications via certified mail so you can track their progress and ensure the VA receives them. Finally, don't send original documents unless you are specifically required to. Instead, see if a certified copy is acceptable; that way, if your application does get lost in the mail, you won't lose those valuable documents as well.

CRITERIA TO QUALIFY FOR VA AID AND ASSISTANCE BENEFITS

To be eligible for the VA's Aid and Attendance benefit program, you must have served ninety consecutive days of active duty, with at least one of the days occurring during one of the following recognized wartime periods:

- World War II: December 7, 1941 – December 31, 1946.

- Korean Conflict: June 27, 1950 – January 31, 1955.

- Vietnam Era: February 28, 1961 – May 7, 1975, for Veterans who served in the Republic of Vietnam during that time, or August 5, 1964 – May 7, 1975.

- Gulf War: August 2, 1990 – through a future date to be set by law or presidential proclamation.[2]

Other eligibility factors depend on your loved one's personal finances and the type of care they need. If your loved one is eligible for these benefits, they can use these funds to offset the cost for the care at home.

WHAT IS THE DIFFERENCE BETWEEN A HOME CARE AGENCY AND A HOME CARE REGISTRY?

The main difference between home care agencies and home care registries is that home care agencies retain a staff of trained caregivers (W-2 employees), while a home care registry is simply a referral source. Home care registries do not directly employ caregivers. Instead, they have contracted with 1099 independent caregivers. Understanding this difference can save you money and protect you from potential legal problems. Here are some components to consider:

CARE PLANS

If you have a home care registry for your loved one, you may still be responsible for knowing what services they need and delegating them to the registry caregiver. However, if you use a home care agency, they are responsible for making sure your loved one receives the services they need from the applicable caregiver. For instance, they will match caregivers to clients based on their personalities and the skill set required.

TAXES AND INJURIES

Hiring a home care registry means you are responsible for reporting and paying the caregiver's taxes and social security. You are also responsible for providing workman's compensation to the caregiver in the event they are injured on the job or in your home. Essentially, the home care registry caregiver is *your* employe and if you fail to fulfill these responsibilities it can result in harsh fines and penalties.

Unlike home care registries, most home care agencies employ W-2 employees, rather than independent contractors. Therefore, your only responsibility is to pay the home care agency directly, not the caregiver. The home care agency will manage their taxes, social security, and any other expenses related to their employment that is required by state and federal governments.

HIRING AND SCHEDULING

When you hire a caregiver from a home care registry, you are responsible for the interviewing and hiring process. You are also responsible for scheduling, so if they call out of work or don't show up, you are responsible for finding their replacement. Alternatively, home care agencies are responsible for scheduling and ensuring reliable and consistent care because they have employees, not independent contractors.

SUPERVISION

Home care agencies manage their employee performance and will perform random supervisory visits to ensure their performance standards are continuously being met. However, if you use a home care registry, you will oversee the caregiver's performance.

THEFT

Home care agencies are typically licensed and insured, and all their employees are bonded. So, if theft occurs, the agency is responsible for making it right. But if you work with a home care registry, and a theft occurs, you are responsible for any losses.

BACKGROUND CHECKS

Unfortunately, not all home care registries conduct a background check on their independent caregivers. To ensure you are hiring a trustworthy and reliable caregiver, you should conduct a background check of your own. If you do not, you might be placing your loved one in unnecessary danger.

Home care agencies, however, do perform background checks on all their employees, screening them for criminal records and licensing issues.

As you can see, there are a number of reasons working with a home care agency is more valuable than working with a home care registry, yet home care agencies tend to be a bit more costly. If working with a home care agency is not in your budget, make sure to find a reputable home care registry and take the time to do your due diligence before hiring one of their independent caregivers. Also, ensure you have the time and resources to stay on top of the independent caregiver once they are performing their duties with your elderly loved ones.

Are You Prepared?

- Taking care of your aging loved ones is difficult to do while continuing to work full time but not impossible. Consider what kind of care they need and where they should live while you care for them. What makes the most sense for your family?

- There are a number of ways to become a paid caregiver. Depending on your loved one's insurance benefits, you might qualify for the Medicaid Cash and Counseling Program, or long-term care insurance.

- Home equity conversion mortgages or reverse mortgages might be a good option for families looking to provide for their elderly relatives when the relative does not have the necessary retirement funds to pay for their care.

CHAPTER 7

FAMILY AND MEDICAL LEAVE ACT

The Family and Medical Leave Act (FMLA) was designed to give employees the time off they need to care for their health or for their relatives. Typically, people associate FMLA with maternity leave. However, it is also available for individuals caring for aging relatives who require specialized care. Over time, many of your employees will have to care for their elderly relatives, but this will require significant time. As such, your employees may need to take a period of leave to care for their loved one.

The best way to help your employees is to allow them to take a reasonable amount of leave to attend to their particular family issues. While this leave is unpaid, FMLA does guarantee that the employee's job will be held for them so they can return to when their leave ends, which will decrease your employee's stress and anxiety considerably. Remember: a secure employee will be a productive employee.

FMLA RULES

The FMLA guarantees an employee's right to take a stipulated period of unpaid leave to provide medical or other types of care for an immediate family member, but there are certain rules that employers must follow when providing FMLA:

1. The FMLA is available for employees to use to care for their own serious health conditions or medical reasons, or those of their spouses, children, or parents.

2. The FMLA leave can be extended up to twelve weeks total.

3. Employees are eligible for FMLA leave if they have worked for the company for at least twelve months, or at least 1,250 hours in the past twelve months, and work at a location where there are at least fifty employees of the same employer within seventy-five miles.[1]

It is important to remember that the twelve-month employment stipulation does not need to be consecutive. Rather, any employment time prior to a continuous break in service of seven or more years does not have to be counted. While the language of the act states that the person must be employed for twelve months, that period does not have to be consecutive. If you have been employed by the same company for twelve months with separations that last no longer than seven years, then that qualifies under FMLA laws. However, you cannot qualify for the twelve weeks of leave if you have taken it within the past year. Additionally, the employee requesting FMLA does not need to work at a worksite with fifty or more employees to qualify. The worksite must employ fifty or more employees who live within seventy-five miles of the worksite.

Basically, the FMLA gives employees the much-needed space and time to find long-term solutions for themselves or their loved ones. However, not all businesses are required to carry FMLA, only certain ones, including:

- Private-sector employers who have had fifty or more employees in the last twenty or more workweeks within the current calendar year or the one before it, including a coveted employer's joint employer or successor.

- Public agencies, including local, state, or federal governmental agencies, regardless of the number of employees it has; or

- Public or private elementary or secondary schools, regardless of the number of employees it has.[2]

HOW TO APPLY FOR FMLA

If you work for a business that carries FMLA, and you qualify for it, applying can seem a little overwhelming. But the first step is always to notify your employer that you would like to take FMLA leave. When you know ahead of time that you will need FMLA, such as for childbirth or adoption, you must give your employer at least thirty days' notice. But if you discover you may need FMLA and can't give them thirty days' notice, your employer just needs to approve it when it is practical—hopefully within one to two days. Additionally, if you discover that you need to take your FMLA leave immediately, and disclosing it to your employer ahead of time is impossible, you need to notify them as soon as you can.[3]

It is important to familiarize yourself with your employer's FMLA leave policy to ensure you are following their specific process properly. This will mitigate any regulatory issues down the line and ensure that you are able to take your leave without any unnecessary hiccups.

Typically, people take FMLA leave:

- To give birth, or help their spouse through birth, and care for the newborn within the first year of their life.

- To adopt or receive a foster child and to care for them within that first year of placement.

- To care for a spouse, child, or parent with a serious health condition.

- To care for their own serious health condition which makes it impossible to perform the essential functions of their job.

Employees can also take FMLA if their spouse, child, parent, or they themselves have been called into active duty to support a contingency operation. Additionally, employees with immediate family members (spouse, child, or parent) who are covered military members can take FMLA to deal with a qualifying emergency that arises out of that family member's covered active duty. And, in some cases, employees may be able to take up to twenty-six workweeks of FMLA leave during a single 12-month period if they need to care for a covered service member with a serious injury or illness.[4]

SPECIAL CIRCUMSTANCES

Unfortunately, there are certain employees who may work for a company required to carry FMLA coverage but still not qualify for it. For instance, certain key employees may not be guaranteed reinstatement in their positions following FMLA leave. The FMLA defines a key employee as a salaried, FMLA-eligible employee who is in the top 10 percent of highest-paid employees who work within seventy-five miles of the same employer's worksite.[5]

In addition, special rules apply to employees of local education agencies. Usually, these rules will only apply when these individuals need intermittent leave or when they need to take their leave near the end of a school term.[6]

The Department of Labor (DOL) amended the definition of spouse so eligible employees in legal same-sex marriages can take FMLA leave to care for their spouse or family member, regardless of where they live.[7]

FMLA Leave Process Flow Chart - See Next Page[8]

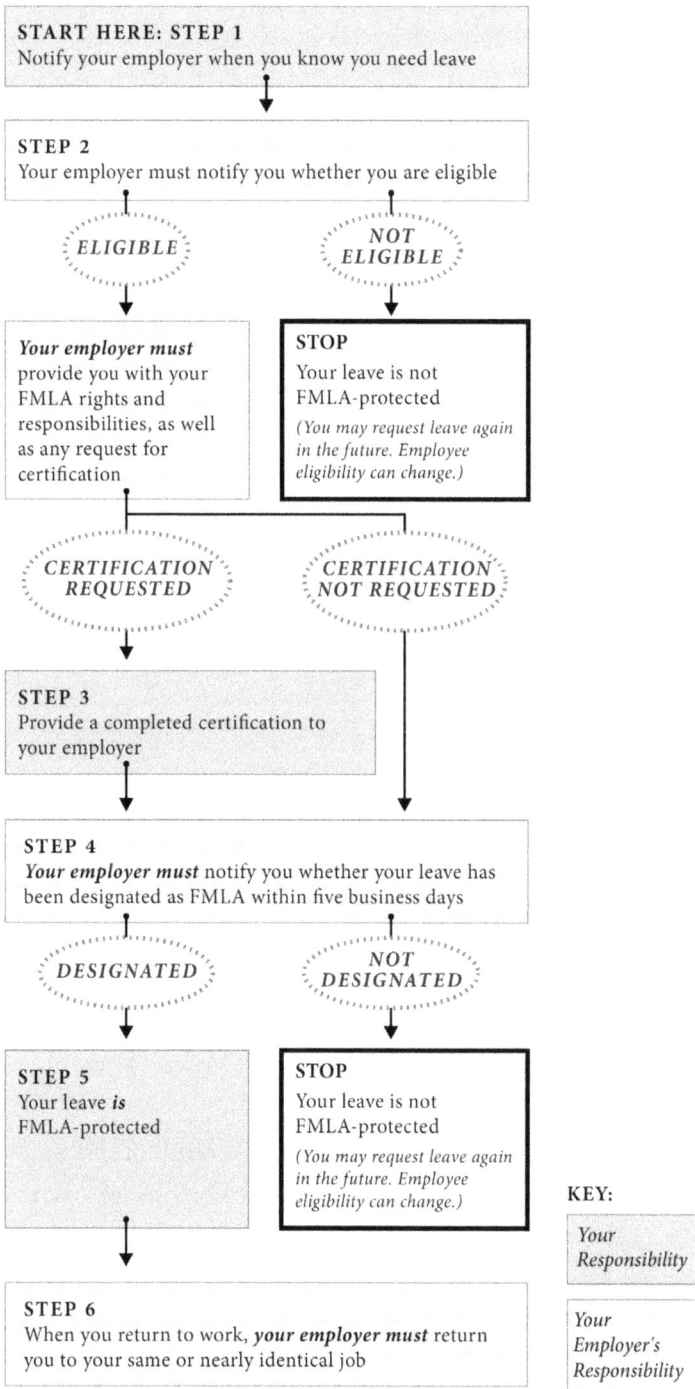

START HERE: STEP 1
Notify your employer when you know you need leave

↓

STEP 2
Your employer must notify you whether you are eligible

ELIGIBLE   *NOT ELIGIBLE*

Your employer must provide you with your FMLA rights and responsibilities, as well as any request for certification

STOP
Your leave is not FMLA-protected
(You may request leave again in the future. Employee eligibility can change.)

CERTIFICATION REQUESTED   *CERTIFICATION NOT REQUESTED*

STEP 3
Provide a completed certification to your employer

STEP 4
Your employer must notify you whether your leave has been designated as FMLA within five business days

DESIGNATED   *NOT DESIGNATED*

STEP 5
Your leave **is** FMLA-protected

STOP
Your leave is not FMLA-protected
(You may request leave again in the future. Employee eligibility can change.)

KEY:

Your Responsibility

Your Employer's Responsibility

STEP 6
When you return to work, **your employer must** return you to your same or nearly identical job

FILING A COMPLAINT

If you think your FMLA rights are being violated, or you simply have questions about the act, you can contact the Department of Labor's Wage and Hour Division (DOLWHD). To file a complaint with DOLWHD, you will need to have the following information on hand:

- Your name
- Your address and phone number
- The name of the company you want to get leave from
- The company's location, which may differ from the actual job site where you worked
- The company's phone number
- The name of the owner or manager
- The circumstances of your FMLA request and your employer's response[9]

While FMLA is an incredible benefit for employees looking to care for themselves or their family members, there are three key points you should be aware of prior to apply for it:

1. The use of FMLA is restricted to care or emergencies for an employee's immediate family. So, for instance, FMLA will probably not cover leave if you want to care for your siblings, in-laws, or grandparents unless those grandparents were once your legal guardian or your sibling is disabled.

2. Legally, a child over 18 is no longer a minor. However, if your child cannot take care of themselves because of a serious medical condition, you are still eligible for FMLA.

3. If your employer provides other types of leave like maternity, paternity, or workman's compensation, you may be able to tack your FMLA leave on to either end of that leave. Moreover, you

will still be eligible to take FMLA even if you are also taking another type of covered leave during that same calendar year.

The point of FMLA is to fill the gaps in employer coverage while ensuring you have the same position to come back to when your leave is over. However, you will want to discuss your FMLA leave with your employer the moment you discover you may need it.

HOW FMLA CAN HELP EMPLOYEES CARING FOR AGING LOVED ONES

As I explained above, FMLA coverage is typically restricted to immediate family unless your grandparent had legal guardianship of you as a child. That being said, there have been a number of complaints that employees who are also family caregivers should be allowed to use their FMLA. Recently, the DOL has clarified that FMLA can be used by employees whose aging loved ones need to complete a respite stay.[10]

WHAT IS A RESPITE STAY?

Respite stay is a short-term stay in a senior living community to allow an elderly individual to recover from a health condition or hospital treatment. The DOL allows employee family caregivers to request an extended vacation or time off from work to care for their elderly loved one during this time. This kind of FMLA is called respite care.

As such, if you do not expressly qualify for FMLA because your aging loved one was not your legal guardian, you may be able to use the respite stay or care as an alternative. This will allow you to not only take the time to care for your aging loved one, but to have peace of mind that your position will still be there when you get back.

WHAT THE POLITICIANS NEED TO UNDERSTAND

Most politicians have a rudimentary understanding of FMLA. Usually, they know that it can be used for maternity or adoption leave, but they are unclear on how the FMLA rules can be extended to other ailing family members. They aren't considering who is going to care for an employee's parent when they break their hip, or the aunt with dementia, or the millennial employee's grandmother that basically raised them after their parents divorced. Even when politicians sponsor bills that would support caregivers, nothing comes to fruition.

The only way for these policies to evolve with the times is for caregivers to speak up. FMLA was originally ratified into law in 1993. It's high time it was updated. And while there is some talk about including the costs of services associated with Medicare into FMLA, that will only help certain seniors get by financially, but it won't help their caregivers.

HOW WILL HEALTHCARE LEGISLATION IMPACT YOUR WORKPLACE BENEFITS?

The uncertainty in today's healthcare legislation causes the cost of healthcare premiums to rise. For instance, in California, officials reported that monthly health insurance premiums could rise 7.9 percent in 2025.[11] Nationwide, healthcare costs are suspected to rise around 8 percent as well.[12] As such, your HR department—and your benefits broker—may start scrambling to minimize these costs to the company, which may inflate your costs upfront.

If your company plans to overcome legislative uncertainty and the rising costs of health care, it's time to put a plan in place to assess how to focus your efforts moving forward. In Chapter 5, we talked about how to use your benefits broker to get the best possible benefits package for your particular employees. To create a plan that overcomes legislative uncertainty, you will need to:

1. Review your current benefits plan annually. Start by compiling a list of all the benefits you offer your employees.

2. Analyze the individual benefit's effectiveness. Just like when you were initiating the original benefits plan with your benefits broker, you will need to conduct annual employee surveys to see which benefits they are using and which they are not.

3. Work with your benefits broker to find plans that are best suited for your company. Consider things like company budget, employee demographics, ease of implementation, and program analytics to ensure your company's ROI improves.

Putting It into Practice

In September, you conduct your annual employee benefits review with your benefits broker. During the review, you discover that benefit A is rarely utilized by your employees. However, it can cost the company $0.90 per employee, per hour, your benefits broker might suggest removing benefit A and replacing it with a more cost-effective program your employees actually need and providing benefit A as an opt-in benefit for the employees who want it.

By creating a review and analysis routine, you can ensure your company does not waste money on ineffective benefits and still provides high-quality, cost-effective benefits that truly support your employees.

Are You Prepared?

- The FMLA guarantees your right to take a certain amount of unpaid leave to provide medical or another type of care for yourself or an immediate family member.

- There are special circumstances that allow specific types of employees to take FMLA. You will want to review these special circumstances to see if your employment falls under one of them and how this will impact your FMLA leave request.

- Healthcare legislation is incredibly volatile and changes all the time. As such, employers should review their current FMLA benefits plan annually and ensure the benefits are not only effective but being utilized appropriately.

CHAPTER 8

TIPS TO GET YOU STARTED CAREGIVING

Becoming a family caregiver is an incredibly wonderful gift, albeit a thankless one. There are so many challenges you will have to learn how to navigate over the coming days, weeks, months, and years. Having the support of your employer is paramount to learning how to overcome these challenges. In this chapter, we will discuss several of the tips I've learned through my years as my own family's caregiver and my professional experience as a caregiving business owner.

ENROLL IN MEDICARE

As a caregiver, you will likely be responsible for enrolling your parents in Medicare. You can help them navigate the enrollment process, but you will need to have their authorization to access their personal health information and discuss their coverage with Medicare providers. This usually involves signing an Authorization to Disclose Personal Health Information form. If you're not familiar with Medicare, here is a little Medicare 101.

The History of Medicare

Recognizing the financial burden of healthcare costs on older Americans, President Lyndon B. Johnson proposed a national health insurance program. On July 30, 1965, he signed into law the bill that led to Medicare and Medicaid. Medicare is the federal health insurance program for people aged 65 and older, to include some younger people with disabilities. It has been a cornerstone program in the United States for over half a century. When Medicare first started in 1966, it consisted of two parts:

Part A (Hospital Insurance): This part covered hospital stays, skilled nursing facility care, hospice care, and home health services.

Part B (Medical Insurance): This part covered doctor visits, outpatient care, medical equipment, and some preventive services.

In 2006 Medicare expanded to include Medicare Part D, which provides prescription drug coverage.

Today, Medicare remains a vital program for millions of Americans. It has helped to reduce poverty among older adults and has improved access to healthcare for many. Medicare faces numerous challenges, including rising healthcare costs and debates over its long-term sustainability.

You should apply for Medicare during your Initial Enrollment Period (IEP). This period typically starts three months before the month you turn sixty-five and ends three months after. If you miss your IEP, you may have to wait for a General Enrollment Period (GEP) or a Special Enrollment Period (SEP) to sign up, and you may face penalties. IEP is the best time to sign up. It starts three months before your sixty-fifth birthday and ends three months after. You may qualify for a SEP if you have certain life events, like losing job-based health coverage or moving to a new area. Now, if you miss your IEP and SEP, you can enroll during the GEP, which runs from January 1 to March 31 each year. However, you may face a penalty. Here are something's you need to consider when you're enrolling. If you're already receiving

Social Security benefits when you turn 65, you'll be automatically en-
rolled in Medicare Part A. You'll need to sign up separately for Part
B. But if you're still working and have employer-sponsored health insurance, you may want to delay enrolling in Medicare Part B. Another
option to consider are Medicare Advantage plans. These are offered by
private insurance companies and often include additional benefits like
vision and dental coverage.

For more detailed information and to apply for Medicare, you can
visit the Social Security Administration website or call 1-800-772-1213.

How to Apply for Medicare

If you're nearing your sixty-fifth birthday or are already eligible for
Medicare due to a disability, here's a general guide on how to apply:

Online: You can apply online through the Social Security
Administration's website (SSA).

By Phone: Call the Social Security Administration at 1-800-772-1213.

In Person: Visit your local Social Security office.

You will need access to certain documents like a birth certificate or
passport to verify age, and a Social Security card or a document with
your SSN on it. You will also need proof of your citizenship or lawful
permanent residency.

Last but not least, you will need your past work history and earnings. Consider a Medicare Advantage plan option. It's important to review your Medicare coverage annually to ensure it meets your needs.
You need to be aware of your monthly premiums, deductibles, and
co-payments. If you have questions or need assistance with the application process, contact your local Social Security office or a Medicare
counselor. If you're considering a Medicare Advantage plan, also
known as Part C, you should know that it provides an alternative to
Original Medicare (Parts A and B). It typically covers all the benefits of

Original Medicare, including hospital stays, doctor visits, and preventive care. Many plans also offer additional benefits like vision, dental, and hearing coverage by offering comprehensive coverage, often including prescription drug coverage (Part D). There are several types of Medicare Advantage plans; each comes with its own rules and costs. There are Health Maintenance Organization (HMO) Plans that, typically, force you to choose a primary care physician (PCP) who will coordinate your care.

You'll most likely need a referral to see specialists. You can expect to pay lower costs for in-network care as opposed to out-of-network. Another plan option is a Preferred Provider Organization (PPO).

You can see any doctor or healthcare provider, but, again, you'll usually pay less for in-network providers. With these types of plans you normally don't need a referral to see a specialist. There plans called Health Maintenance Organization-Point of Service (HMO-POS) that are a hybrid of an HMO and PPO plans. These types of plans you can see out-of-network providers, but you'll pay higher costs. Then there are the private fee-for-service plans (PFFS). These are similar to Original Medicare, but with additional benefits and rules set by the insurance company. Everything has its pros and cons, so you just need to sit down (annually) with your Medicare adviser and discuss your needs and let them find what's best for you.

Some of the Pros in the all-in-one coverage plans include Part D prescription drug coverage.

Additional benefits: Some plans offer extra benefits like vision, dental, and fitness programs.

Potential cost savings: Depending on the plan, you may have lower out-of-pocket costs. Some of the Cons come with network restrictions. You may need to choose doctors and hospitals from a network.

Some plans may have higher monthly premiums than Original Medicare. Some may have complex rules and regulations that are hard to understand and can be challenging. When choosing a Medicare Advantage plan, again sit down with your agent/adviser and consider your needs. Think about your health conditions, prescription drug needs, and preferred doctors and hospitals that you like. Compare all the plans that are offered and consider the costs. It's always best to go through an agent; however, if you care to do it on your own, please use the Medicare's official website (Medicare.gov) to compare plans in your area. There is a lot of fraud out there. To summarize, talk to your doctor and discuss your healthcare needs and any specific medications you take. Consult with a Medicare adviser. They can help you understand your options and help you make an informed decision. Remember: It's important to review your Medicare Advantage plan annually to ensure it continues to meet your needs. Finding a good agent or broker that you can work with is key to saving money and adding the right benefits.

Disclaimer: This information is intended for general knowledge and informational purposes only, and does not constitute professional advice. Please consult with a qualified healthcare professional or financial adviser for advice tailored to your specific circumstances as Medicare changes annually.

HOSPITAL TIPS FOR SENIORS AND FAMILY CAREGIVERS

Prior to heading to the hospital with your senior family member, there are a few things you should keep in mind:

1. **Pick the right hospital.** Make sure you pick a hospital within your loved one's insurance network that they are familiar with and that their primary physician can practice at. Keep in mind that freestanding ERs and urgent care centers may have lower wait times, but they typically have less equipment, which some senior health conditions will require.

2. **Try to schedule surgery early in the week.** While you may not always have the luxury of scheduling surgeries ahead of time, if you did, hospitals have more staff, doctors, and nurses available during the workweek between 9 a.m. and 5 p.m. than they will outside those times. Aiming for an appointment at the beginning of the week will ensure your family member gets ample care.

3. **Remember: germs are *everywhere*.** *Wash in and wash out!* Hospitals are filled with germs. Make sure anyone entering the room sanitizes their hands before coming in and as they leave. Do not rely on the hospital to have sanitized everything. There are countless stories of elderly patients coming in to the hospital with one ailment only to contract pneumonia, MERSA, or some other infection during their stay.

4. **Communication is key.** Don't be afraid to speak up. Ask for a list of physicians and nurses who will be taking care of your loved one in the hospital. Talk to all the doctors and see if you can be a part of their end-of-shift handover. You should request to be in your loved one's room when this takes place.

5. **Doctors are motivated.** Hospitals are not the most profitable businesses, so doctors and administrators are motivated to provide surgeries to bring more money into the hospital. As such, before agreeing to a surgery, ask for a second independent opinion to ensure that the surgery or procedure is actually necessary.

6. **Understanding and controlling costs.** Find out if your loved one is going to be admitted to the hospital or if they'll be under observation. This is a critical clarification because Medicare won't pay for post-hospitalization services like rehab or home health care unless your loved one has been admitted to the hospital for at least three days. In addition, make sure to check your loved one's hospital bills because four out of five bills typically have errors that can cost your loved one extra.[1]

7. **Carry a list of their medications.** Always bring a printed list of your loved one's medications, even over-the-counter medicines to ensure there are not complications or interactions with the medicines the hospital might provide. The medication list should be clear and include the full drug name, dosage amount and time of day, and any other special instructions.

8. **Compare rehabs.** Usually, rehabilitative care can be performed at home or in a facility. If your physician orders your loved one to rehab in a facility, just know that you do not have to go the facility the physician ordered. To ensure you have the right fit, it is important to call different facilities in your area to discuss the type of care your loved one might be needing, and make an impromptu pop-in to check them out ahead of time. The same goes for instances where your loved one's physician prescribes home health care and a particular agency.

WHAT TO DO BEFORE DISCHARGE

Taking notes throughout your loved one's hospital stay is helpful, but taking notes during discharge is especially important. Most hospitals want to discharge a patient before the weekend arrives, so they will not only be coming in and out repeatedly, they will be talking quickly. Even someone with the best memory will find it difficult to remember all the things the medical staff tell you. Write everything they say down.

Additionally, you may not get copies of everything you need from the hospital. So, make sure to request everything before you leave, including copies of all labs, tests, scans, surgery reports, medications, and the discharge summary.

Finally, before you leave, try to schedule your loved one's future doctor appointments. Sometimes, it can be harder to get an appointment once your loved one leaves the hospital. If you insist on making it while you are there, the hospital administrators and nurses may be able to arrange it more quickly.

SPECIFIC TIPS FOR THE SANDWICH GENERATION

If you are one of the many employees in the sandwich generation who are tasked with providing support for their children and elderly loved ones, here are a few tips to ensure you can move into this role more easily:

- Organize: You will need to organize your time so you can make the most out of each day.

- Prioritize: Once you have organized your time, you will need to figure out which tasks you have to tackle and in which order.

- Identity: It is easy to lose your identity when you start caregiving.

With all the responsibilities on your plate, you will want to prioritize what is most important to you as an individual. Establishing and maintaining your identity is vital to your success in supporting your family.

- Stress: One of the biggest hurdles to overcome as a caregiver is stress, especially if it feels like there is no end in sight. The increased stress associated with caregiving can negatively impact even the healthiest individual. Getting enough rest, prioritizing self-care, and engaging in a new workout routine or mindfulness practice are easy ways to ensure you can reduce as much stress as possible while continuing to provide the best care you can. As they say, you can't pour from an empty cup.

- Assistance: Caregiving is an immense burden, especially when the caregiver is juggling multiple roles and working to provide for their family. No person should have to bear this burden alone, so accept help when you can to make things easier. And remember, help comes in several forms. Sometimes its hiring someone to do the grocery shopping for you, and other times it's allowing a friend to help with the laundry. In other cases, it is requesting assistance and resources from your employer. The more companies realize what their employees need, the more they will move in the direction of providing support services to enable their employees to get back to work.

HAVING DIFFICULT CONVERSATIONS WITH YOUR LOVED ONE

There are many difficult conversations you will have with your family as they age, but few are as brutal as telling a parent or grandparent they can no longer drive their vehicle. For most adults, a vehicle represents

independence, allowing a person to go where they want, when they want, without relying on anyone else. As such, many elderly loved ones are upset when it is taken away. I had one client whose aging mother refused to give up her driver's license, despite her faculties beginning to slow. It wasn't until the second time she drove through a grocery store window that they finally put their foot down.

With nearly fifty million seniors in the US, more and more people over the age of sixty-five are on the road. It's no question that at some point these seniors have to stop driving themselves, but when? There is no federal law in place that requires them to be retested based on their ability, and each state has its own mandate for seniors. So, what are the signs you need to look out for to encourage your aging loved one to hand over the keys?

The best way to evaluate your parent's driving capability is to get in the car with them and have them drive to a routine destination. As they drive, look out for:

- Slow reactionary times.

- Driving slower than normal traffic.

- Getting lost along the way.

- Having trouble parking between the lines.

Other things to look for are dents or dings that "appear out of no-where" on the vehicle or a habit of losing their keys. If you notice any of these things, you might want to have your loved one's driving ability retested. When having this conversation, it helps to avoid the issue of their age and instead focus on specific areas of their driving ability that has changed. Many causes of changes to their driving abilities are not just age; more often than not it is impaired vision, medication use, or other limiting mental or physical conditions that are affecting their ability to drive.

When I was with my father, I would typically be the one driving. However, one day, I asked him to drive to the store and explained to him that I didn't remember how to get there. While he was driving, I noticed he wasn't taking the highway. Instead, he stuck to the back-roads. I told him I was glad he was driving because I thought the store had been off the highway. That's when he told me he was uncomfortable driving on the highway. On backroads, he could go at his own pace. I didn't have any issues with his driving until we got to the store, and he parked in two spots and backed out without looking behind him as he did.

I called the DMV the next day and explained that my father shouldn't be driving. The lady at the DMV told me to download a form for his doctors to fill out and return it to the state DMV Division. Two months after turning in the form to the DMV, I received a message that they would not be revoking my father's license. I immediately called the DMV and spoke to a supervisor who told me that they were there to protect the rights of their citizens, not take them away. I explained that I wasn't trying to take away my father's right to operate a vehicle so much as protect other people on the road that he might harm with his impaired driving. When I was finished, there was a long pause at

the other end of the line before the supervisor informed me that my father's license expired in two months and if he did not renew it on time,
he would have to take another driving test to reinstate it.

Though this was not the outcome I had hoped for, it does show
how reactive we are as a society. Even when a caregiver tries to be proactive, a government body can get in the way and prevent them from
caregiving to the best of their abilities. What if my elderly father had a
seizure while driving, veered off the road, and hit a stone fence, injur-
ing himself and his passenger? In that case, the DMV would likely have
suspended his license until he started some sort of seizure medication.
Though maybe they would have also made him retake a driving test
and note the medication necessity on their driver's license—like how
many licenses state whether the driver wears contacts or glasses. In this
case, the license suspension or revocation would have had to do with a
medical condition and not his age.

However, if your aging loved one can no longer drive safely and
you need to take their vehicle away from them, make sure you offer
them alternatives to getting around so that they can maintain some
sort of independence and freedom (and probably soften the blow!).
Alternatives to driving include:

- Bus

- Train

- Taxi

- Uber or Lyft

- Paratransit

- Family and friends

- Personal driver

Of course, which alternatives you offer will depend on the area
your loved one resides in. Public transportation is inexpensive but limited and time-consuming in most areas, and taxi or ride-shares may

offer direct transportation, but they are usually more expensive. And in some cases, your loved one may be embarrassed to rely on family, friends, or companions to drive them around. Before talking to your loved one, make sure you have a feasible plan in place so that they are more at peace with the decision to stop driving.

In instances where your loved one is upset about the prospect of turning in the keys, you will need professional help. Acting as caregiver is already a new type of relationship with your loved one and can get in the way of expressing how important it is for them to stop driving. Your parent has always parented you, and now it may feel like they are being parented by you. Having a professional with insight into the problem, and how loved one's typically respond to such requests, can be so helpful. Try getting help from their physician, optometrist or ophthalmologist, or attorney. Even your state's Department of Motor Vehicles can help by providing relevant statistics and information.

In the end, unfortunately, if your loved one's driving poses a danger to others on the road, you will have to take their keys away regardless of how they respond to your discussion. It's not just their life at risk, but the lives of so many others that should guide your actions.

WHEN IS THE RIGHT TIME FOR YOUR LOVED ONE TO DOWNSIZE OR MOVE?

We spend so much of our lives complaining about how our home isn't big enough, only to discover one day that we don't need all this extra room anymore. Aging individuals will likely decide to downsize once they have this realization and then move to a smaller home or eldercare facility. But if they aren't coming to this realization, you may need to bring it up.

As there is no magic age or state or federal regulation that stipulates when someone needs to downsize, here are some things to look out for to determine whether downsizing is necessary:

- There's too much stuff taking up space that could be donated or thrown away.

- They have unused rooms.

- Your loved one lives too far from family or friends, making it difficult for them to participate in their family events, recitals, or sports games. When this happens, elderly individuals can feel isolated, which may create even more issues for their mental and physical health.

- Maintaining the home and yard is difficult for your loved one to do alone.

When you or your loved one decides it is time to downsize or move into an elderly facility, having a plan is key. Start by going through all the items in the home, donating and selling what you can, and tossing what you don't want or need.

Additionally, before you place the house on the market, make sure you know where your loved one is going. Are they coming to live with you or another family member? Are they going to rent or buy something smaller in a 55+ community? Are they interested in senior care centers, assisted-living facilities, or nursing homes? Have you checked them out yet?

Wherever they are moving to, it needs to fit them. If they can still care for themselves, then a smaller living space is fine. But if they need more assistance, they should be moving in with family or friends, getting home care or companion care, or moving into a senior care facility where these things are provided around the clock.

ENSURING LOVED ONES REMAIN CONNECTED

Seniors have spent their whole lives providing for themselves. Realizing that they need an official caregiver may not be the easiest step for many of them. As such, many of your elderly loved ones may start suffering from depression or anxiety. To try and combat the realities of aging, it is important to ensure they see their family and friends whenever possible. Keep their world big and it can prevent them from succumbing to the stressors of aging.

MAKE A TO-DO LIST

Becoming a caregiver is overwhelming, and the best thing you can do is have a plan. But like all overwhelming things, creating a plan can feel tantamount to climbing Mount Everest—where do you even begin? I've outlined a simple to-do list below to get you started. Before taking on any caregiver responsibilities, make sure they have these items in place:

1. **Medical POA**. Have your loved one designate someone to make healthcare decisions on their behalf.

2. **Durable POA**. Have them designate someone to make financial and legal decisions on their behalf.

3. **Living Will or Trust**. If your loved one has assets, they should have a living will or trust that includes these assets and describes how they should be delineated and when, to avoid having to attend probate court.

4. **Emergency Contacts**. Make sure to have a list of individuals that can reach your loved one in case of an emergency if you live too far to get their first.

5. **Access to Banking Information**. To ensure there is no fraud or abuse on their accounts, you will want to gain access to their banking information early on.

A legacy and wishes planning system like Future File (discussed on page 32) will ensure users have these key items available and organized when they are needed.

It may be best to begin with a visit to the primary care physician (PCP). Follow up enough with your loved ones to show you care and don't overwhelm them. Let them work at their pace, but gently guide them in the importance of things. Maybe it's time to discuss with close family members who could be the primary family caregiver point of contact.

THE MISSION AND SERVICE OF THE FAMILY CAREGIVER ALLIANCE

If you are currently struggling to hold a full-time job while also taking care of an aged or ill relative, know that you are not alone. Being a primary caregiver is a full-time job on top of the career you already have, and it can certainly be overwhelming. As such, the Family Caregiver Alliance (FCA) has created a series of unique resources for caregivers in need of assistance.

The FCA was founded in the 1980s by a group of families and community leaders in the San Francisco area. It created a network of special care and support for patients who suffered from conditions that did not fit into the normal health care system at the time, like Alzheimer's, Parkinson's, and other traumatic injuries and disorders. The FCA's goal has always been to provide resources that improve the quality of life for patients and their caregivers. It fulfills this mission by disseminating helpful information, providing special services, and tirelessly advocating for caregivers and patients across the nation.

Further, the formation of the FCA has created lasting results, including the birth of an entire California-wide network of Caregiver Resource Centers. Since then, a national alliance of caregivers has evolved to address the needs of both patients and their caregivers. For example, the FCA works closely with the Bay Area Caregiver Resource Center, offering caregivers special consultation services to help them devise a plan for the long-term care and treatment of the relatives they are caring for. The organization has been developed to serve families in San Francisco and its immediate metro area, including San Mateo, Santa Clara, Alameda, Contra Costa and Marin counties.

WHAT IS THE NATIONAL CENTER ON CAREGIVING?

The National Center on Caregiving (NCC) is the arm of the FCA that engages in special research and advocacy to integrate caregivers into the national health and social services system. The NCC also provides info and resources to policymakers to help them craft programs and initiatives that give family members the assistance they need to transition into the role of full-time caregivers.

The NCC has a special Caregiver Policy Digest e-publication and webinars that provide further information on its activities and future goals. Present and future caregivers should take advantage of this resources as much as possible.

Understanding how to caregive efficiently takes time. Most caregivers are thrust into their situation with little to no preparation. But the most important thing to remember is to give yourself grace, take it day by day, and lean on your support system. Make sure you know what your employer offers in terms of eldercare benefits, and if they don't have any, make sure you tell them why they are necessary. The only way your employer will be able to meet your needs is if you inform them of them.

NOW WHAT?

You just finished this book and you're wondering, "Does this really affect my business?"

The facts—as old and outdated as they are—are the facts. America is aging, and there is nothing we can do to stop it. Caring for a loved one is not a matter of "if" but "when." Leaders that have not gone through caring for a loved one don't know what the others are up against. You don't know what the future holds. No one plans on falling and breaking a hip, it just happens and then their loved ones have to step up and deal with it.

We are a reactive society, and our reactivity results in higher employee absenteeism, lost productivity, and even lost wages and retirement, which affects employees of all ages. It creates a financial burden for both businesses and their employees.

So, how can businesses help? Be proactive. Face this crisis head on. Don't look the other way because this isn't something that will go away.

This book was written for C-Suite, Human Resource Administrators, small business owners, and employee benefit companies—anyone that wants to make change within their organization by being proactive. The journey of a proactive leader is a continuous one. It requires courage, resilience, and a relentless pursuit of excellence. By embracing this philosophy and mindset, you can unlock your full potential and make a lasting impact on the world. Today, now more than ever, businesses need proactive leaders. It's time to step up, seize opportunities, and drive positive change. Let's embrace the challenges, overcome obstacles, and shape a brighter tomorrow. Let us inspire others, innovate fearlessly, and build a better future together. Thank you. God Bless.

CONSULTING INQUIRIES

Scot Cheben is available for consulting with business leaders and human resource managers on this growing crisis. Eldercare is impacting employees and, in turn, affecting workplace productivity within respected companies. Scot partners with organizations to assist leadership in achieving a better understanding of current policies they have in place and assist in creating and implementing new policies that can support their employees' caregiving efforts, and thus the organization's bottom line. If you haven't experienced being a caregiver, it can be hard to understand what your company is truly up against. To learn more about how Scot can help you and your valued team members navigate the eldercare maze, please visit eldercareleader.com. There, you can take the risk assessment quiz and schedule a free fifteen minute, one-on-one consult, to review the report with him and see if your company is at risk. Scot is also available via email at: scot@eldercareleader.com.

ENDNOTES

1   Chabeli Carrazana, "Caregiving Costs Women Nearly $300,000 in Lost Pay over Their Lifetimes, Department of Labor Finds," The 19th, May 11, 2023, https://19thnews.org/2023/05/caregiving-women-parents-children-cost-lifetime/.

2   Family Caregiver Alliance, "Caregiver Statistics: Work and Caregiving," Family Caregiver Alliance, 2016, https://www.caregiver.org/resource/caregiver-statistics-work-and-caregiving/.

3   Jen Loginov, "The Aging of America: A Changing Picture of Work and Retirement," Georgetown Center for Retirement Initiatives, March 22, 2018, https://cri.georgetown.edu/the-aging-of-america-a-changing-picture-of-work-and-retirement/.

4   Pew Research Center, "Baby Boomers Approach 65—Glumly," Pew Research Center's Social & Demographic Trends Project, December 20, 2010, https://www.pewresearch.org/social-trends/2010/12/20/baby-boomers-approach-65-glumly/.

Chapter One

1   "United States," AARP International, n.d., https://www.aarpinternational.org/initiatives/aging-readiness-competitiveness-arc/united-states.

2   U.S. Census Bureau, "Older People Projected to Outnumber Children," The United States Census Bureau, December 3, 2018, https://www.census.gov/newsroom/press-releases/2018/cb18-41-population-projections.html.

3   Beth Baker, "Caregivers Incur Higher Health Costs for Selves," Workforce.com, September 1, 2010, https://workforce.com/news/caregivers-incur-higher-health-costs-for-selves.

4   Denise Brodey, "73% of Employees Have a Secret Second Job—It's Caregiving," Forbes, April 25, 2024, https://www.forbes.com/sites/denisebrodey/2024/04/25/73-of-employees-have-a-secret-second-job-its-caregiving/.

5   Alzheimer's Association, "New Alzheimer's Association Report Reveals Top Stressors for Caregivers and Lack of Care Navigation Support and Resources," Alzheimer's Disease and Dementia, 2024, https://www.alz.org/news/2024/facts-figures-report-dementia-caregiver-stress.

6   AARP, Jo Ann Jenkins, CEO, "More than 10 Million Millennials Are Caregivers," AARP, n.d., https://www.aarp.org/caregiving/home-care/info-2018/millennial-caregivers-work-life.html.

7   Family Caregiver Alliance, "Caregiver Statistics: Demographics," Family Caregiver Alliance, 2016, https://www.caregiver.org/resource/caregiver-statistics-demographics/.

8   "Aging in America—Institute on Aging," Institute on Aging, March 6, 2015, https://www.ioaging.org/aging-in-america/.

9   Ibid.

10   Juliana Menasce Horowitz, "More than Half of Americans in Their 40s Are 'Sandwiched' between an Aging Parent and Their Own Children," Pew Research Center, April 8, 2022, https://www.pewresearch.org/short-reads/2022/04/08/more-than-half-of-americans-

in-their-40s-are-sandwiched-between-an-aging-parent-and-their-own-children/.

11   Ibid.

12   "Unpaid Eldercare in the United States—2015-16 Summary," Bureau of Labor Statistics, 2015, https://www.bls.gov/news.release/elcare.nr0.htm.

13   "National Caregivers Day—Alzheimer's Tennessee, Inc. — Support, Education and Research for Alzheimer's Disease and Related Dementias," Alzheimer's Tennessee, n.d., https://www.alztennessee.org/events/annual-events/national-caregivers-day.

14   Mayo Clinic, "Practical Solutions for Caregiver Stress," Mayo Clinic, March 22, 2022, https://www.mayoclinic.org/healthy-lifestyle/stress-management/in-depth/caregiver-stress/art-20044784.

15   Moira Fordyce, MD, MB, and ChB, "Caregiver Health," Family Caregiver Alliance, n.d., https://www.caregiver.org/resource/caregiver-health/#20.

16   Si-Sheng Huang, "Depression among Caregivers of Patients with Dementia: Associative Factors and Management Approaches," World Journal of Psychiatry 12, no. 1 (2022): 59–76, https://doi.org/10.5498/wjp.v12.i1.59.

17   Barry S. Oken, Irina Fonareva, and Helane Wahbeh, "Stress-Related Cognitive Dysfunction in Dementia Caregivers," Journal of Geriatric Psychiatry and Neurology 24, no. 4 (2011): 191–98, https://doi.org/10.1177/0891988711422524.

18   Selena Caldera, Susan Reinhard, Ari Houser, and Rita Choula, "Estimating the Economic Value of Family Caregiving at a National and State Level," Innovation in Aging 7, Supplement_1 (2023): 241–41, https://doi.org/10.1093/geroni/igad104.0793.

19   Phyllis Mutschler, "Women and Caregiving: Facts and Figures," Family Caregiver Alliance, 2015, https://www.caregiver.org/resource/women-and-caregiving-facts-and-figures/.

20   Keita Fakeye, Maningbè B. Laura J. Samuel, Emmanuel F. Drabo, Karen Bandeen-Roche, and Jennifer L. Wolff, "Caregiving-Related Work Productivity Loss among Employed Family and Other Unpaid Caregivers of Older Adults," Value in Health: The Journal of the International Society for Pharmacoeconomics and Outcomes Research 26, no. 5 (2023): 712–20, https://doi.org/10.1016/j.jval.2022.06.014.

21   "2023 Study—Caregiving in America, Statistics on Family Caregivers and Beyond | Guardian," Guardian Life, n.d., https://www.guardianlife.com/reports/caregiving-in-america.

22   Juliana Menasce Horowitz, "More than Half of Americans in Their 40s Are 'Sandwiched' between an Aging Parent and Their Own Children," Pew Research Center, April 8, 2022, https://www.pewresearch.org/short-reads/2022/04/08/more-than-half-of-americans-in-their-40s-are-sandwiched-between-an-aging-parent-and-their-own-children/.

23   "NCHS Pressroom—1995 Fact Sheet—Advance Report of Final Divorce Statistics," Centers for Disease Control and Prevention, May 24, 2019, https://www.cdc.gov/nchs/pressroom/95facts/fs_439s.htm.

24   AARP, Jo Ann Jenkins, CEO, "More than 10 Million Millennials Are Caregivers," AARP, n.d., https://www.aarp.org/caregiving/home-care/info-2018/millennial-caregivers-work-life.html.

Chapter Two

1   The MetLife Study of Caregiving Costs to Caregivers, "Double Jeopardy for Baby Boomers Caring for Their Parents," 2011, http://

www.caregiving.org/wp-content/uploads/2011/06/mmi-caregiving-costs-working-caregivers.pdf.

2   "Medicaid   Cash   and   Counseling   Programs,"
Medicaidplanningassistance.org, 2019, https://www.medicaidplanningassistance.org/question/medicaid-cash-and-counseling-programs/.

3   "14.3 Million Americans Are Military Caregivers; Burden Falls
Heaviest on Those Caring for People Aged 60 and Younger," RAND
Corporation,   September   24,   2024,   https://www.rand.org/news/
press/2024/09/24.html.

4   Nancy Kerr, "Family Caregivers Experience High Out-of-Pocket
Costs," AARP, June 29, 2021, https://www.aarp.org/caregiving/financial-legal/info-2021/high-out-of-pocket-costs.html.

5   AARP, "New AARP Survey Finds Life Is Good, Especially for
Older   Americans,"   MediaRoom,   2024,   https://doi.org/10211431.
rev202410211431.

6   K.E. Covinsky et al., "Patient and Caregiver Characteristics
Associated with Depression in Caregivers of Patients with Dementia,"
Journal of General Internal Medicine 18 (2003): 1006-14; Alzheimer's
Association & National Alliance for Caregiving, Families Care:
Alzheimer's Caregiving in the United States (Chicago, IL: Alzheimer's
Association and Bethesda, MD: National Alliance for Caregiving,
2004).

7   C.R. Pierret, "The Sandwich Generation: Women Caring for
Parents and Children," Monthly Labor Review, September 2006.

8   Phyllis Mutschler, "Women and Caregiving: Facts and Figures,"
Family Caregiver Alliance, 2015, https://www.caregiver.org/resource/
women-and-caregiving-facts-and-figures/.

9   Richard Eisenberg, "The Financial and Personal Toll of Family Caregiving," Forbes, March 12, 2018, https://www.forbes.com/sites/nextavenue/2018/03/12/the-financial-and-personal-toll-of-family-caregiving/#4cf748f758b8.

10   Ibid.

11   Leo Almazora, "Survey Highlights Financial Challenges across Generations as Longevity Increases," Investmentnews.com, October 23, 2024, https://www.investmentnews.com/retirement-planning/survey-highlights-financial-challenges-across-generations-as-longevity-increases/257833.

12   "Social Security Benefits Planner: Retirement," Social Security Administration, https://www.ssa.gov/planners/retire/r&m6.html.

13   Maddie Duley, "Here's How Much Americans Are Saving in 2023 vs. 2022," Yahoo Life, March 27, 2023, https://www.yahoo.com/lifestyle/americans-savings-stack-2023-vs-140023973.html.

14   "This Is the Average 401(K) Balance for Retirees Age 65 and Older," Nasdaq.com, 2024, https://www.nasdaq.com/articles/average-401k-balance-retirees-age-65-and-older-1.

15   Ibid.

16   James Royal, "What Is the Average Social Security Check?" Bankrate, March 23, 2023, https://www.bankrate.com/retirement/average-monthly-social-security-check/.

17   "Income from Pensions," Pension Rights Center, n.d., https://pensionrights.org/resource/income-from-pensions/.

18   Tina Hurley, "Key Takeaways," Citizens, 2024, https://www.citizensbank.com/learning/how-much-money-do-you-need-to-retire.aspx.

19 "1 in 3 Americans Has $0 Saved for Retirement," Nasdaq.com, March 14, 2016, https://www.nasdaq.com/articles/1-3-americans-has-0-saved-retirement-2016-03-14.

20 Genworth, "Cost of Long Term Care by State | 2018 Cost of Care Report | Genworth," Genworth.com, 2018, https://www.genworth.com/aging-and-you/finances/cost-of-care.html.

21 Ibid.

22 Ibid.

23 Ibid.

Chapter Three

1 "US Average Hourly Earnings," Ycharts.com, n.d., https://ycharts.com/indicators/us_average_hourly_earnings.

2 "Unpaid Eldercare in the United States—2017-2018 Data from the American Time Use Survey," Bureau of Labor Statistics, n.d., https://www.bls.gov/news.release/pdf/elcare.pdf.

3 "How Providing Caregiving Affects Your Workforce," AARP Employer Resource Center, September 17, 2024, https://employer-portal.aarp.org/build-expertise/how-providing-caregiving-affects-your-workforce/.

4 Mark Mather and Paola Scommegna, "Fact Sheet: Aging in the United States," Population Reference Bureau, January 9, 2024, https://www.prb.org/resources/fact-sheet-aging-in-the-united-states/.

5 Ibid.

6 Administration for Community Living, "National Family Caregiver Support Program | ACL Administration for Community

Living," 2016, https://acl.gov/programs/support-caregivers/national-family-caregiver-support-program.

7   Ibid.

8   The Lancet Healthy Longevity, "Care for Ageing Populations Globally," The Lancet Healthy Longevity 2, no. 4 (2021): e180, https://doi.org/10.1016/s2666-7568(21)00064-7.

9   Felix Richter, "Infographic: The World's Oldest Populations," Statista Infographics, February 20, 2023, https://www.statista.com/chart/29345/countries-and-territories-with-the-highest-share-of-people-aged-65-and-older/.

10   "'Better Life Better Place' for the Elderly and Children Program," The Nippon Foundation, September 16, 2021, https://www.nippon-foundation.or.jp/en/news/articles/2021/20210916-62312.html.

11   Shuichi Nakamura, "Japan's Welfare for the Elderly— Past, Present, and Future," Asia Health and Wellbeing Initiative, December 1, 2018, https://ahwin.org/japans-welfare-for-the-elderly-past-present-and-future/.

12   "Italy – Eurocarers," Eurocarers, n.d., https://eurocarers.org/country-profiles/italy/.

13   "Dementia Village Hogeweyk in the Netherlands," Be Advice EN,   n.d.,   https://www.bethecareconcept.com/en/hogeweyk-dementia-village-hogeweyk-netherlands/.

14   "Help and Information," Carers.org, n.d., https://carers.org/help-for-carers/introduction.

15   "Deep Dive: China's Elderly Population Is Rising, but There Aren't Enough Carers," Young Post, February 25, 2024, https://www.scmp.com/yp/discover/article/3252846/deep-dive-chinas-elderly-population-rising-low-pay-lack-advancement-means-there-arent-enough.

16 "Alzheimer's and Related Disorders Society of India," ARDSI.org, 2024, https://ardsi.org/.

17 "What is Snoezelen?" Snoezelen Multi-Sensory Environments, accessed February 19, 2025, https://snoezelen.info/.

Chapter Four

1 Bureau of Labor Statistics, "Employer Costs for Employee Compensation—September 2016," 2024, https://www.bls.gov/news.release/pdf/ecec.pdf.

2 "5 Awesome Job Benefits That Attract Quality Candidates," Glassdoor.com, 2021, https://www.glassdoor.com/blog/5-job-benefits-attract-quality-candidates/.

3 Ibid.

4 Amazing Workplaces, "Netflix's Exceptional Parental Leave Policy: A Model for Inclusivity," September 12, 2023, https://amazingwork-places.co/netflixs-exceptional-parental-leave-policy-a-beacon-of-sup-port-and-inclusivity/.

5 "Parental Leave Is Not a Vacation, but It Is a Blessing," HR Blog, n.d., https://hrblog.spotify.com/2023/11/22/parental-leave-is-not-a-vacation-but-it-is-a-blessing-strong.

6 "Asana Employee Benefits | Built in NYC," Builtinnyc.com, 2022, https://www.builtinnyc.com/company/asana/benefits.

7 "Selected Long-Term Care Statistics | Family Caregiver Alliance," Caregiver.org, 2019, https://www.caregiver.org/selected-long-term-care-statistics.

8   Ashley Autry, "Employee Benefits and Perks Statistics - the Ultimate Collection," Accessperks.com, Access Perks, January 7, 2019, https://blog.accessperks.com/employee-benefits-perks-statistics.

9   "2012 National Study of Employers," Balancing Work and Family Care of Older Persons, July 6, 2012, https://fyi.extension.wisc.edu/balancingcare/2012/07/06/2012-national-study-of-employers/.

10   "The Good News about Eldercare Benefits at Work," FE Parker Dev, January 2015, https://feparkerdev.azurewebsites.net/blog/january-2015/the-good-news-about-eldercare-benefits-at-work.

11   Cloey Callahan, "Pet Insurance Rises as a Hot New Workplace Benefit," WorkLife, December 5, 2023, https://www.worklife.news/culture/pet-insurance-benefit/.

12   "How Much Is Pet Insurance in 2024?" NerdWallet, January 10, 2024, https://www.nerdwallet.com/article/insurance/cost-of-pet-insurance.

13   "Wagmo Employee Pet Benefits," Wagmo.io, 2022, https://wagmo.io/business/blog/pet-perks-benefits.

Chapter Five

1   2024 Senior Report,⊠ America⊠s Health Rankings, accessed December 2024, https://assets.americashealthrankings.org/app/uploads/ahr_2024seniorreport_comprehensivereport.pdf.

Chapter Six

1   "VA Aid and Attendance Benefits and Housebound Allowance." 2020. Veterans Affairs. September 24, 2020. https://www.va.gov/pension/aid-attendance-housebound/.

2   "Veterans Aid and Attendance Benefit Eligibility | VeteranAid. org." 2021. VeteranAid. February 2, 2021. https://www.veteranaid.org/ aid-and-attendance-eligibility.php.

Chapter Seven

1   U.S. Department of Labor. 2023. "Fact Sheet #28: The Family and Medical Leave Act | U.S. Department of Labor." www.dol.gov. February 2023. https://www.dol.gov/agencies/whd/fact-sheets/28-fmla.

2   Ibid.

3   Fact Sheet #28E: Employee Notice Requirements under the Family and Medical Leave Act | U.S. Department of Labor." n.d. www.dol.gov. https://www.dol.gov/agencies/whd/ fact-sheets/28e-fmla-employee-notice.

4   U.S. Department of Labor. 2023. "Fact Sheet #28: The Family and Medical Leave Act | U.S. Department of Labor." www.dol.gov. February 2023. https://www.dol.gov/agencies/whd/fact-sheets/28-fmla.

5   "29 CFR § 825.217 - Key Employee, General Rule." 2014. LII / Legal Information Institute. 2014. https://www.law.cornell.edu/cfr/ text/29/825.217.

6   Canaday, Chelsea. 2023. "Employment Law Reminder for Educational Entities—Consider Special Rules within FMLA, FLSA, and Title IX - HR Blog." HR Blog. May 2023. https://hr.dickinson-wright.com/2023/05/01/employment-law-reminder-for-educational-entities-consider-special-rules-within-fmla-flsa-and-title-ix/.

7   "A Rule by the Wage and Hour Division," National Archives Federal Register, February 25, 2015, https://www.federalregister. gov/documents/2015/02/25/2015-03569/definition-of-spouse-under-the-family-and-medical-leave-act#p-3

8   Graphic adapted from "The FMLA Leave Process," The US Department of Labor, accessed February 19, 2025, https://www.dol.gov/agencies/whd/fmla/FMLA-leave-process.

9   As the DOL regularly updates its regulations, this is just a guide. Prior to making a complaint, you need to familiarize yourself with the current policy and potentially retain legal counsel to ensure eligibility.

10   "Fact Sheet #28C: The Definition of 'Parent' as It Applies to an Individual Who Stood in Loco Parentis to an Employee for FMLA 'Eldercare' Protections. | U.S. Department of Labor." n.d. www.dol.gov. https://www.dol.gov/agencies/whd/fact-sheets/28C-fmla-eldercare.

11   "Covered California's Rates and Plans for 2025: The Most Financial Support Ever to Help More Californians Pay for Health Insurance." 2024. Coveredca.com. 2024. https://www.coveredca.com/newsroom/news-releases/2024/07/24/2025-rates-and-plans/.

12   PWC. 2019. "Behind the Numbers 2019: Healthcare and Medical Cost Trends: PwC." PWC. 2019. https://www.pwc.com/us/en/industries/health-industries/library/behind-the-numbers.html.

Chapter Eight

1   Gooch, Kelly. 2016. "Medical Billing Errors Growing, Says Medical Billing Advocates of America." www.beckershospitalreview.com. April 12, 2016.

ABOUT THE AUTHOR

Scot is a well-respected entrepreneur in the elder care industry who spent his early life working in aeronautics before owning his own home care business. He is a national keynote speaker for the eldercare industry as well as an instructor in dementia care.

Scot first encountered the challenge of balancing caregiving with employment in 2008 when his father suffered a heart attack. There was no company policy for supporting caregiving employees he could not find the help he needed for his father. Realizing the growing need for caregivers, and the lack of employer guidance or awareness, he dedicated his life and career to aiding the eldercare industry.

In 2011 he owned a home care franchise, Senior Helpers, which supplied highly trained caregivers to help the elderly live independently in their home. In 2014, he co-founded the Senior Providers Network to help educate caregivers and guide them to the right resources. This experience helped him transition into a career in the eldercare industry.

www.ingramcontent.com/pod-product-compliance
Lightning Source LLC
Chambersburg PA
CBHW050823090426
42738CB00020B/3460